THE STONE CARVERS

MASTER
CRAFTSMEN OF
WASHINGTON
NATIONAL
CATHEDRAL

THE
STONE
CARVERS

MARJORIE HUNT

SMITHSONIAN INSTITUTION PRESS   WASHINGTON AND LONDON

Designer: Linda McKnight

Library of Congress Cataloging-in-Publication Data
Hunt, Marjorie, 1954–
The stone carvers : master craftsmen of
Washington National Cathedral / Marjorie Hunt.
p.   cm.
Includes bibliographical references and index.
ISBN 1-56098-829-0 (alk. paper)
1. Morigi, Roger, 1907–1995.   2. Palumbo, Vincent,
1936–   .   3. Stone carvers—United States—Biography.
4. Washington Cathedral.   I. Title.
NB237.M613H86   1999
730'.92'273—dc21
[B]   99-19958

British Library Cataloguing-in-Publication Data available

Printed in Italy, not at government expense
06 05 04 03 02 01 00   5 4 3 2

∞   The paper used in this publication meets the mini-
mum requirements of the American National Standard for
Information Sciences—Permanence of Paper for Printed
Library Materials ANSI Z39.48-1984.

For permission to reproduce illustrations appearing in this
book, please correspond directly with the owners of the
works, as listed in the individual captions. The Smithsonian
Institution Press does not retain reproduction rights for these
illustrations individually or maintain a file for addresses for
photo sources.

Frontispiece: Stone carvers Frank Zic, Roger Morigi, and
Vincent Palumbo pose in the niches of Washington National Cathedral.
(Photo by Morton Broffman)

page iv: South portal tympanum and voussoir angels, Washington
National Cathedral. (Photo by Robert C. Lautman)

page vi: Birds tease a cat frozen in a stone column on the north side
of Washington National Cathedral. (Photo by Robert C. Lautman,
courtesy of Marjorie Hunt)

page vii: The trumeau statue of Saint Paul on the west facade of
Washington National Cathedral, designed by sculptor Frederick Hart
and carved by Vincent Palumbo. (Photo by Brooks Photographers)

FOR MY FATHER AND MOTHER
IRA AUGUSTUS HUNT JR. AND MERRY T. HUNT

This book has
been made possible
through the
generous support of
The National
Italian American
Foundation
in honor of
Domenic F. Antonelli Jr.
whose grandfather,
Andrew E. Bernasconi,
was a stone carver

CONTENTS

ACKNOWLEDGMENTS

I owe a great debt of gratitude to stone carvers Roger Morigi and Vincent Palumbo for so generously sharing their knowledge, skills, stories, and friendship with me. Their voices, and their passion for their craft, resound in these pages. I would also like to acknowledge stone carvers Constantine Seferlis, Frank Zic, John Guarente, and Patrick Plunkett for their fine artistry and their important contributions to this study; the Very Reverend Francis B. Sayre Jr., dean emeritus of Washington National Cathedral, for his thoughtful insights and assistance; and Louise Morigi and Mary Lou Palumbo for their warm and gracious hospitality.

This book has been shaped and inspired at every turn by the pioneering work of my great teacher and mentor, Henry Glassie. His critical thinking and writings illuminated my research and influenced the presentation of my findings. I am deeply grateful for his valuable advice and guidance and for his wonderful encouragement and support throughout. I also owe a great debt of gratitude to my teachers Barbara Kirshenblatt-Gimblett and Dell Hymes, whose key perspectives on performance, communication, and expressive tradition greatly influenced my work, and to Kenneth S. Goldstein, whose kind and constant help guided me toward the completion of my doctoral degree in folklore at the University of Pennsylvania.

Bosses on the vaulted ceiling of Washington National Cathedral. (Photo by Robert C. Lautman)

I wish to express my deepest appreciation to the National Italian American Foundation, whose generous support in honor of Domenic F. Antonelli Jr., a founding member and longtime supporter, has made this book possible. I am especially grateful to Alfred Rotondaro, the executive director of the National Italian American Foundation, for his enthusiastic interest and support and for his untiring advocacy for the beauty and value of Italian American culture, history, and art. My sincere thanks also go to Maria Lombardo, the director of education programs, and Dona De Sanctis, the director of research and cultural affairs.

I particularly wish to thank my colleagues at the Center for Folklife and Cultural Heritage at the Smithsonian Institution for their encouragement and help. I began my research with the stone carvers at Washington National Cathedral while conducting fieldwork for the 1978 Festival of American Folklife. I am especially grateful to Ralph Rinzler, who believed in and assisted me with this project from the beginning; to Richard Kurin, the director of the center, who provided me with invaluable support and words of encouragement; and to Betty Belanus, Linda Benner, Olivia Cadaval, Rich Kennedy, Diana N'Diaye, Diana Parker, Jeff Place, Pete and Arlene Reiniger, Peter Seitel, Stephanie Smith, Barbara Strickland, Tom Vennum, and Cynthia Vidaurri for their wonderful friendship and collegiality. I also want to extend my warmest thanks to Paul Wagner, my friend and collaborator on *The Stone Carvers,* our documentary film about the stone carvers of Washington National Cathedral, and to my dear friend Mary Hufford, who has been a source of great inspiration and support throughout.

I would like to thank Joseph Alonso, Robert Becker, Daphne Figuerero Gerig, Joanne Lawton, Donovan Marks, and Don Myer at Washington National Cathedral for their valuable support and assistance with this project. I also am especially grateful to Richard Hewlett, the historiographer of the Washington National Cathedral Archives, Jesse Wilson, the photo archivist, Richard T. Feller, the canon clerk of the works emeritus, and Nancy Fetterman, the former assistant clerk of the works, for their kind and knowledgeable help.

This book could not have been realized without the commitment and expertise of several people at the Smithsonian Institution

Press: Mark Hirsch, senior editor, American studies; Daniel Goodwin, former director; Ruth Thomson, editor; and Linda McKnight, designer. To them I extend my sincerest thanks and heartfelt appreciation.

Most of all, I am grateful to my wonderful family—my parents and siblings, my husband, Allen Carroll, and my daughters, Tess and Grace—for their love, help, and understanding. I could not have completed this book without them.

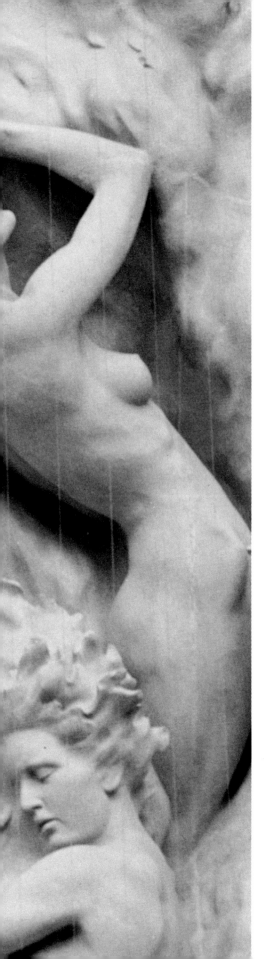

INTRODUCTION
WORKING THE STONE

You cut and cut and all of a sudden you see something grow. The more you work, the better it comes out. You feel good inside. You work, it gets brilliant, you see it move. I don't know, it fills you with some kind of emotion—such a sense of satisfaction.

ROGER MORIGI, MASTER CARVER

rom the Gothic cathedrals of Europe to the Beaux-Arts skyscrapers of New York, stone carvers have brought enduring beauty to our built environment, creating works of art that bear the touch of human hands and hearts. This is the story of two great masters of the craft, Roger Morigi and Vincent Palumbo, stone carvers at the Cathedral Church of Saint Peter and Saint Paul in Washington, D.C., more popularly known as Washington National Cathedral. It is the story of their great pride and creative spirit, their love for their work, and their commitment to excellence, manifested in lasting works of beauty in stone.[1]

Roger Morigi and Vincent Palumbo, craftsmen of exceptional artistry and skill, have been heirs to the accumulated knowledge and technical mastery of generations of stone workers in their families and local communities. Both were born and trained in Italy. Roger's father, Napoleone Morigi, was an ornamental carver from the north of Italy who worked in the United States at the turn of the century, carving decorative works for the Library of Congress and other monumental

Detail of the Creation tympanum on the west facade of Washington National Cathedral, designed by sculptor Frederick Hart and carved by Vincent Palumbo with the assistance of Patrick Plunkett, Gerald Lynch, and Walter Arnold. (Photo by L. Albee)

Master stone carver Roger Morigi worked at Washington National Cathedral from 1956 until his retirement in 1978. (Photo by Morton Broffman)

buildings in Washington, D.C., and New York. Roger followed in the family tradition, training with old-time masters in the carving workshops of Viggiu, Italy, and attending the renowned Accademia di Belle Arti di Brera in Milan.

In 1927 Roger immigrated to the United States, where he worked as a stone carver for more than half a century, leaving his mark on many of our nation's most important public buildings. In 1956 he began his long and distinguished career at Washington National Cathedral, serving as the Cathedral's master carver for twenty-three years. Roger died in 1995 at the age of eighty-seven, but the spirit of creativity and excellence that infused his work lives on in a monumental legacy in stone—the magnificent works of art he left behind.

Vincent Palumbo followed in Roger's footsteps, becoming the

Cathedral's master carver in 1978. A fifth-generation stone carver, steeped in a rich tradition of stone carving going back centuries in his region, Vincent learned his craft from his father and grandfather in their family shop in Molfetta, Italy, before immigrating to the United States in 1961. An accomplished master in his own right, Vincent has worked at the Cathedral for thirty-eight years—more than half his lifetime—carving the hundreds of sculptures and decorations that are an integral part of Gothic design, creating works of art that bear the imprint of his mastery and skill.[2]

Like Roger before him, Vincent deeply values his family heritage and his occupational skills, and he is proud of the long and vital history of his trade. "Even God," he told me, "even God gave Moses the ten laws on stone. He carved the Ten Commandments on stone. So this is the oldest trade in the world!"[3]

Vincent Palumbo, an Italian American master stone carver, has worked at Washington National Cathedral for thirty-eight years. (Photo by Paul Wagner)

Washington National Cathedral, a fourteenth-century English Gothic style cathedral, overlooks Washington, D.C., from the city's highest point, Mount Saint Alban. (Photo by Morton Broffman)

For both these craftsmen the past has been "powerfully operative" in the present, influencing the way in which they have viewed themselves and have performed their craft.[4] Their art has connected them to their families, to their fellow carvers and their work community, and to the greater tradition of stone carving of which they are a part, binding them to past and future generations, providing them with a way to measure themselves and to connect meaningfully with others.

My study looks to the carvers' "shaping past"—to their background, training, and development in the craft in the context of their families, local communities, and the carving workshops where they served their apprenticeships.[5] I document the stone-carving process—the carvers' methods, materials, tools, and techniques—and explore the formative forces that underlie craftsmanship—the ideas, attitudes, values, traditional rule systems, and notions of beauty and excellence that the carvers bring to their work.[6]

Memory and tradition are critical shaping factors in workmanship—as influential on the carvers' actions as events in the present.[7] When Vincent Palumbo carves, for example, his father's teachings and his vivid memories of the many years they spent working together guide and inspire his actions. "When I was working with my father on a job," he told me, "we don't feel we were father and son, but just partners. We talk a variation of things—how to do the best. He always teach me the secrets how to give the master touch, how always he wants me—even if stone is a dead material—still he was telling me how to make that stone look like life, almost talk, look realistic. Especially to give that small detail, so when we were carving flowers, the petals of the flowers look like moving. That was the *best* part. And I'm trying to do the best I can in his memory."

Looking to the carvers' biographies and training—to their early education and development in the craft—revealed many of the crucial elements of skill that lie at the core of the creative process and yet are "hidden in the performer's mind."[8] As anthropologist Gregory Bateson points out, "The fact of skill indicates the presence of large unconscious components in the performance."[9] Interviewing Roger and Vincent about their experiences and training, getting them to reflect on the learning process, and listening to their personal narratives—key texts that encapsulate not only important attitudes and principles but also information on technology and process—helped me to understand and to appreciate the complexity and depth of the carvers' skill: their special abilities and techniques; their extensive knowledge of tools, materials, and methods.

Stone carvers view themselves as performers, as creative individuals engaged in the skillful act of interpretation. Through their knowledge, skills, and abilities, their judgment and care, they transform a design on paper or in clay into a lasting work in stone. In their work they are less concerned with design, with the creation of new texts, than they are with technique, with ways of working the stone. Their emphasis is on artistic action, on the process of creation. What matters is the performance of skill.[10]

Roger Morigi and Vincent Palumbo have shared a deep appreciation for the aesthetic value and expressive power of technical perfection.[11] They have delighted in skill and have found meaning and pleasure in the poetic qualities of workmanship—in their ability to manipulate the tools and materials of their trade and to create objects of beauty through their special "touch," through the mastery of technique.[12] "You cut and cut and all of a sudden you see something grow," said Roger. "The more you work, the better it comes out. You feel good inside. You work, it gets brilliant, you see it move. I don't know, it fills you with some kind of emotion—such a sense of satisfaction."

Stone carvers find individual expression through the performance of skill, but they also work within the boundaries of certain culturally determined rules of appropriate behavior and acceptable expression, balancing personal creativity with "group needs and received ideas."[13] Their work is shaped and evaluated by what folklorist Robert McCarl terms a "critical canon" of technique, by shared ideas of what good work should be like.[14]

In the context of the workshop, surrounded by carvers of all levels of skill and ability, they continually watch one another, comparing individual styles and techniques, measuring themselves and evaluating the work of others, striving for the respect and recognition accorded to mastery.[15] "Between ourselves we *knew,* " said Roger Morigi, "we recognized the one who was doing very good, and we would say it, 'Oh, you should see the beautiful work he's doing.' And you wanted that, to hear that, and you wanted to be one of them." Vincent Palumbo put it this way: "First there was the challenge between the stone and myself and also there was the challenge to stay on pace with them [the other carvers in the shop] because they were old masters and they were to judge." Irish stone carver Seamus Murphy

The Majestus, the centerpiece of the Cathedral's high altar reredos, was designed by sculptor Walker Hancock and carved by Roger Morigi with the assistance of Frank Zic. (Photo by Morton Broffman)

spoke for many when he described the thrill of watching a virtuoso performance in stone: "To see that man working was a treat. He made stone-cutting look simple and you wonder why the blazes you had to serve seven years to it. I don't know how he did it, but he had a system of working which left everyone standing."

Stone carvers attend to craftsmanship: to systems of working and ways of touching the stone, to the selection and the use of tools and the treatment of raw materials, to the ordering of actions and the creative decisions and choices that are made as they transform a block of stone into a cultural artifact. In the end the completed carving stands as an "emblem of the creative act," an incarnation of valued experience imbued with memories and meaning.[16]

This concept of craftsmanship as performance—as "cultural behavior for which a person assumes responsibility to an audience"— is crucial to understanding the stone-carving process and its meaning in the carvers' lives.[17] Stone carvers have control over the process of creation, and thus the aesthetic possibilities of an object lie completely in their hands, not only in terms of their skill and ability, but also in terms of their attitudes and intentions. In workmanship we see both the communication of competence and, to use Kenneth Burke's phrase, the "dancing of an attitude"[18]—an elaborate and carefully crafted performance of identity, experience, and values.

Taking my cue from the carvers, in this study I look to the expressive dimension of skill—to the ways in which stone carvers communicate shared ideas, personal creativity, and cultural experience through workmanship.[19] I seek to understand the craft of stone carving from the perspective of the carvers. What do they know and value? How do they perceive themselves and their art? What underlying skills and aesthetic attitudes shape and give meaning to their work?

I began my research with Roger Morigi and Vincent Palumbo and their coworkers at Washington National Cathedral—Frank Zic, Constantine Seferlis, John Guarente, and Patrick Plunkett—in 1978 while conducting fieldwork for the Smithsonian Institution's Festival of American Folklife. Over the course of nearly two decades, I visited the carvers in their homes and at the Cathedral—in the carving workshop, up on the scaffolding, and around the building site. I observed and documented their work techniques and processes, their social interactions, and their verbal lore. I interviewed them about their lives, their training, their aesthetic ideals, and their community traditions. I photographed their work environment and the stone-carving process—their tools, materials, and finished works.[20]

These great craftsmen were my teachers: they guided me on a journey into their world of work, introduced me to a new realm of knowledge and experience, and inspired me with their dedication and their commitment to excellence. The following pages resound with their voices—with their memories, stories, and experiences; their values, aspirations, and ideals. I hope that this book does justice to their story—to their extraordinary skill and artistry, to their pride in their heritage, and to their love for their craft—and that it calls attention to the untold stories of countless other master artisans like them, who for centuries have enriched our world with the work of their hands, leaving a lasting legacy of human excellence for future generations.[21]

1. TRADITION

I come from generations. My father was a stone carver. My grandfather was a stonecutter. So practically there was no apprenticeship for me. I was growing in the trade.

VINCENT PALUMBO

or centuries stone carving has been a traditional craft passed down through the generations from father to son and from master to apprentice. Often the trade was associated with certain families long connected with the craft. Sons followed in their fathers' footsteps, apprenticing to the same local shop masters or joining their fathers and grandfathers in the family stone business.[1] "In Italy, that kind of work, it goes traditional in families," Vincent Palumbo said. "You learn from the father to the son. That's the way it was in those days, to follow the tradition. Every family, every father, was like that."

Tradition is an "actively shaping force," Raymond Williams has written, "powerfully operative in the process of social and cultural definition and identification."[2] A dynamic and selective process, it has a strong incorporating power, bringing forward valued aspects of the past to serve in the present and shaping deeply felt human values into meaningful expressive forms.[3]

Stone carvers work in a granite shed in Barre, Vermont, circa 1902. Many of the stone carvers in Barre hailed from Viggiu, Italy, the same town in Lombardy where Roger Morigi started to learn his craft. (Courtesy of the Archives of Barre History, Aldrich Public Library, Barre, Vermont)

For stone carvers Roger Morigi and Vincent Palumbo, whose roots in the craft reach back generations in their families and local communities, tradition has played a critical role in the acquisition of skills and values: it has shaped their attitudes toward work, informed the way they have defined and identified themselves, and guided the way they have performed their craft. From childhood stone carving was a vital, integral part of daily life and work in their families and small hometowns in Italy. "Practically, I was born into the stone," said Vincent. "I never had any concept to do anything else. I'm a descendant of that trade."

"It's got a lot to do with the section where you come from," said Roger, when I asked him how he started in the trade. "Where I come from in the northern part of Italy, we have a lot of quarries, stone quarries. The main industry was stone, and most of the children would go for that. And another reason, the father would be in the stone business, and the children would follow the stone business. They would follow in their fathers' footsteps."

Inspired by their families, by the rich material legacy of the landscape, and by the long-standing occupational heritage of their local communities, Roger and Vincent's early education and development in stone carving took place in the context of everyday life. In the piazza and on the streets, outside the church and in the public garden, while sitting around the dinner table and visiting with friends—the carvers' early training grounds existed wherever people gathered to talk and to exchange news.

Vincent was born on September 10, 1936, in Molfetta, a fishing port on the Adriatic Sea in the province of Bari in southern Italy. Located near the ancient Appian Way, Molfetta is an old Apulian seacoast town. Its medieval quarter is a maze of narrow, winding streets lined with bleached white limestone buildings. The towers of a thirteenth-century Romanesque cathedral rise up at the edge of the sea. "The port is an elevated piazza upon which stands the old cathedral," noted H. V. Morgan in *A Traveler in Southern Italy,* written in 1969, eight years after Vincent immigrated to America.

> Hundreds of painted boats, each one named after a saint, deposit in the shade of that noble building all the curiosities of the Adriatic Sea. . . . Large blocks of stone have been tumbled into the sea

at the end of the jetty to break the force of winter gales, and these have formed rock pools in which small boys bathe and catch crabs and shrimps in the seaweed, while in the background, as dazzling as if carved in chalk, rise the twin towers of the cathedral seen against the winding warrens of the old town and reflected in the small rock pools.[4]

Vincent described the Molfetta of his youth as a busy town of about 60,000 inhabitants.[5] In his day, he said, the majority of people made their living from fishing or farming, drawing sustenance from both the earth and the sea. "My town, we've got the coast, the sea. We have fishermen. But then we have a lot of farms, too, inside, cultivating the land. Most of this is olives and almonds. That's the main source in our town, agriculture and fish."

In addition to fishing and farming, Molfetta, like many of the other seacoast towns in the region, also supported a variety of small industries, including several brick factories, a steelworks, a few boat-building yards, and an active stone industry. "We have our own local stone which is very good for construction," explained Vincent. "And that's what I've been trained on, this hard stone."

The entire coastal region of central Apulia is rich in limestone, which has been used for centuries by the local people to build their towns, cathedrals, castles, monuments, and homes. "The local limestone with which all the ancient buildings are constructed has been bleached by centuries of sunlight to the whiteness of chalk," noted H. V. Morgan of the distinctive look of the Apulian landscape—a sun-drenched land of barren limestone hills and arid pastures, of gray-green olive groves, rock-filled meadows, and a sparkling azure sea.[6]

"Where I come from, every village has their own kind of stone," said Vincent. "My mother's town, Giovinazzo, has a certain kind of limestone good for making balustrades and balconies. The stone is pretty soft, but a little bit harder than the limestone we have in America. In my town, in Molfetta, we have a stone which is a little bit harder than the one in Giovinazzo. And in Trani we have the best stone—that's stone, not marble—in all of Italy, *pietra di Trani,* which they send all around the world."

In Vincent's time Molfetta had about four or five active quarries and perhaps a dozen stone shops, most of them small- to medium-

Vincent Palumbo, age three, dressed as St. Anthony. (Courtesy of Vincent Palumbo)

sized family operations. "They were all around the city," remembered Vincent. "It depend on where the boss, the little company, can find some land." These shops specialized primarily in stonecutting work: crafting moldings, pediments, balconies, pavement stones, tomb chapels, and the like. Still, said Vincent, "every shop had a couple of carvers" to fashion figures and ornamental details when needed. "In Italy, where I come from, if anybody build a house or villa, there was always carving, always a little art. And so they call for the carver."

On a small plot of land near the outskirts of Molfetta, Vincent's grandfather, Nicholas Palumbo, had his stone shop, a small business that had been passed down in the family over five generations. "We've always been independent," Vincent proudly told me. "America's the first time in five generations that we work for someone else."

Nicholas was a master builder and stonecutter. Vincent's father, Paul Palumbo, was the artistic master, a stone carver and sculptor. Together they ran the family shop. Vincent described the division of work and responsibility this way: "My grandfather was more an architectural person, you know, in building, especially artistic work like monuments in the city for some high, famous people in my hometown, or building artistic tombstones, building tomb chapels in the cemetery with statues all around. All things like that. And my father was the sculptor and the carver. He used to do all the decoration. And so they working together. My grandfather was the man in charge, and my father was the man in charge, too, but more in the artistic line, in ornamental stuff."

An independent master, Nicholas employed anywhere from two to twelve journeymen stonecutters, depending on the amount of work in the shop. Of those, many were family members. "Mainly it was my grandfather, my father, and me," said Vincent, "but also my grandfather's nephew, my brother-in-law, my brother-in-law's father, my brother Nick, and sometimes my uncle on my mother's side, a couple of cousins, and some strange people, too. It all depend on how big the job was. First we keep in consideration members of the family—they came first."

Vincent's grandfather was a well-known and highly respected master in Molfetta. A patriarch of sorts, he had taught many of the local stoneworkers their trade. "Most of the shop masters, they come out from my grandfather. They had great respect for him. They all used to call him 'Master Nick.' 'Master Nicola,' in dialect." Although Vincent only remembered the times when at most ten to twelve stonecutters worked in his grandfather's shop, his brother-in-law, Matteo Dejennaro, ten years his senior, recalled earlier days "when stone was at its peak" and as many as twenty-five stonecutters worked in the shop. "He had a big yard," Matteo told me, "with lots of work, lots of people."

Born in 1906, Vincent's father was from all accounts a carver of masterful abilities. "My father, in five generations, he reached the highest level of the art," said Vincent with pride. Matteo told me, "He was number one. There was nobody else! He have his art inside his

Paul Palumbo carves a statue of Archangel Michael for Washington National Cathedral, circa 1962. (Photo by Stewart Bros. Photographers)

blood. There's not too many people like that." Both men described how stone carvers in their hometown would visit the local cemetery just to view Paul's beautiful work. "He carved a memorial with a little bird, a coat of arms, and a little chain, a flexible chain that moved," said Vincent of a legendary tombstone that his father carved when he was only twenty-one years old. "It was so small, so delicate. No one could believe it! It's in the cemetery in Molfetta, and lots of carvers, they would go to see it. They couldn't believe it. They thought it was an imitation—a [real] chain painted white."

In addition to sculpting and carving his own designs, Paul also carved the work of local sculptors. "My father was the only sculptor *and* carver in my hometown," Vincent told me. "We had a big international sculptor who was my father's teacher, but he was not a carver, he just model [clay]. And even him, when he have work, he calls my father. He didn't trust nobody to do his work on marble, on stone, except my father. Because my father, besides to be a sculptor on clay, he knew how to work marble, he knew how to work stone, because my grandfather was a stoneman."

The Palumbo family shop specialized in ornamental stonework. They built massive tomb chapels and carved elaborate tombstones. They crafted monuments for the town square, made statues for local churches and public gardens, and carved decorative details such as family crests and intricate moldings for neighboring villas and municipal buildings. "You go to Molfetta, and you go in the garden, the city garden. There is a bronze monument over there to the unknown soldier—an angel with wings spread out helping the soldiers—and all the base, the stone base, was done by my grandfather and my father," said Vincent.

Although the occasional commission for a piece of sculpture or a civic monument came their way, the great majority of work done by the Palumbo family, especially after World War II, was for the local cemetery. "After the war, who could afford to have a monument or a statue? So most of our work, it was on tombstones," said Vincent.

In keeping with the style and custom of the day, the tomb chapels and gravestones crafted by the Palumbos, particularly those built for the wealthier families in their province, could be quite elaborate. "The old tombstones which we did in those days, they're standing tall over there," said Vincent, with obvious pride. He described working with his father and grandfather on tomb chapels—stone mausoleums in which entire families were buried—that were as large as fifteen feet square and two levels deep and were adorned with intricately carved altars, pediments, cornices, and other decorative details.

Tombstones could be just as elaborate, with all manner of ornamental carvings and numerous bas-relief sculptures. "The tombstones are not like over here—just a piece of granite," said Vincent. "They were in marble, maybe two meters long by sixty centimeters tall. You get maybe two- to three-centimeter relief. You got to do in miniature. A lot of the people wanted the scene of how a person died. That sometimes involved as many as seven or eight figures."

Despite the Palumbos' reputation for excellence, times were hard, and jobs were difficult to come by. Like centuries of journeymen stone carvers before them, Vincent's grandfather and father were forced by necessity to lead nomadic lives, "following the stone" in search of work.[7] As a young man Nicholas worked on building projects in at least six countries. "My grandfather was a very good master. In his youth he been to a lot of countries," related Vincent. "He spent ten or fifteen years in Russia under the czar. He was building over there, and he was there during the revolution. My grandfather used to speak seven or eight languages. He'd been to Russia, Bulgaria, Germany, Yugoslavia, Romania. As a matter of fact, my father was born in Yugoslavia!"

Vincent's father followed a similar pattern, struggling to make ends meet and to support his family. His search for work took him to Egypt, Ethiopia, and eventually the United States, where he immigrated in 1956 and lived until his death in 1966.

When Vincent—the second youngest of five children—was born in 1936, Paul and his wife, Nicolette, were living in Molfetta where, in addition to working in his father's shop, he had established a small carving studio of his own. "My father's studio was located on the main street," said Vincent. "The main street is like a *corso*. At one end is the railroad station, and on the other end is the sea, and before the sea is the *villa* with the public garden. And the people on Sunday they walk all the way up and down the street and meet their friends. And on both sides of the street were shops, and that's where my father had his

Vincent Palumbo, age fourteen,
Molfetta, Italy, 1950. (Courtesy of
Vincent Palumbo)

studio. He had about three or four guys, and he did a lot of work over there."

By the late 1930s Paul began traveling to Ethiopia, then under Italian occupation, to work for extended periods. Alone much of the time, Nicolette decided to move the family to her hometown of Giovinazzo, a small fishing village four miles south of Molfetta, where Vincent spent much of his childhood and youth. When World War II broke out, Paul was called back from Ethiopia to enlist in the Italian army. He was later taken prisoner by the British and did not return home until 1945.

When he returned from the war, Vincent's father opened a little carving studio in Giovinazzo. "I remember almost the first work he did when he come back from war," recalled Vincent. "I think he did the relief of the Last Supper. That was the first work he did. And after that he did a statue of the Immaculate Conception." Some of Vincent's most cherished memories are of those early days with his father in the little carving studio in Giovinazzo. "I was a little kid, maybe nine years old, and after school, instead of leaving me on the street to play, he took me with him in the shop. And I had to start to clean the shop for the other people who work in the shop and start to look how the other people working, and so I get involved like that."

Vincent's mother died in 1947, when he was eleven years old. After her death Paul moved his shop back to Molfetta, although he and his children continued to live in Giovinazzo. "He got back together with my grandfather in the same shop," said Vincent, "and they worked together." By this time Vincent had completed his formal schooling, and he began to work full time in the family stone business, riding his bicycle daily from Giovinazzo to Molfetta and back, helping his father and grandfather with whatever needed to be done. Strong bonds between father and son, between family and work, were forged in the shop in those early days.

Vincent worked with his father and grandfather in their shop in Molfetta for nearly ten years. Then, in 1956, Paul immigrated to the United States, joining his eldest son, Nick, and other family members in White Plains, New York. "My brother was the base," said Vincent of the Palumbo family's pattern of migration. "My father used to work in New York City. And there were three or four big stone yards nearby—huge shops for stone, for milling stone, for sculpturing and carving work. And my father used to find jobs through these big stone shops."

As stone-carving jobs became increasingly difficult to find in the New York area, Paul moved to Washington, D.C., where stone carvers and cutters were needed to work on the restoration and re-modeling of the U.S. Capitol. "In Washington they were remodeling part of the U.S. Capitol," recalled Vincent. "So my father came to Washington to work on the Capitol. He carved—there's a panel near the entrance with two or three figures and an eagle—and my father carved the eagle. When the Capitol was finished, the Shrine [of the Immaculate Conception] was at the building stage. So he went to the Shrine. Then he joined the Cathedral in 1959. They needed carvers."

Vincent remained in Molfetta, helping his grandfather run the family shop until Nicholas's death in 1961. Paul returned to Italy to help Vincent close the shop, and then together they journeyed back to America, where Vincent, to his great joy, was once again reunited with his father at Washington National Cathedral. "My father, since I can remember in Italy, we always work together, me and him," Vincent told me. "More than father and son, it was more or less just friends. Because since the first day I started to clean the shop until the day he left for America, we always working together. And then, even when I came over to the United States, I get back with him again, and I stayed with him until he died in 1966. Right here at the Cathedral."

Born into a family of stoneworkers, Vincent grew up steeped in the trade. Learning the craft came with being in the family; it was an integral part of everyday life and experience, a part of growing up. "How I learn, I'm growing," said Vincent, "because I come from gen-erations. My father was a stone carver. My grandfather was a stone-cutter. So practically there was no apprenticeship for me. I was growing in the trade."

Vincent was nourished by a constant flow of ideas and talk about work; his education in the craft began, and continued to take place, in the home, in the discourse of daily life. "When you come from a tradi-tional family," he said, "you learn from the talking. What happened to me, we was in that trade. We was talking about work anytime; at breakfast, dinner, supper, most of the subject was work. Think about

Archangel Michael, designed by sculptor Granville Carter and carved by Paul Palumbo, peers down from its niche in the south transept of Washington National Cathedral. (Photo by Stewart Bros. Photographers)

this stone, how we gonna do this, who was gonna do that, we gotta use this trick. So you're growing, and you listen, and your mind, it gets drunk with all those things, and then, when it comes time, you remember."

The importance of the family as a key teaching institution is echoed in the experiences of other traditional artisans.[8] In his memoir, *Stone Mad,* Irish stone carver Seamus Murphy expressed it this way: "I used to hear my father talking about the craft every evening of his life. He would talk about it for hours to my mother, and she was interested in it, too, because all her people were in the trade, and she knew nearly as much as he did. I remember well when I went to work first, how much I already knew about it. I was familiar with all the tools and the terms the men used about stone. 'Twas just the same as home to me."[9]

For Vincent a crucial foundation was laid during that early, informal period of learning.[10] Like a child learning language, he began to acquire a grammar of stone carving; he began to piece together knowledge of the various elements of the craft and the underlying principles that governed them. Sitting around the dinner table listening to his father and grandfather tell stories and discuss work, he became familiar with the names of the tools and the different types of stone. Little by little, he became acquainted with the work processes and specialized terminology of the trade. He began to get a sense of the structure of working relationships, both inside and outside the family shop, all the while absorbing ideas about what good work should be like, until, as he says, his mind became "drunk with all those things." Vincent brought this reservoir of knowledge to the shop when he began to work with his father and grandfather.

At the same time that Vincent was gaining knowledge about the technical aspects of stone carving, he was also learning about the importance of the craft to his family. The stories he heard about his great-grandfather, his grandfather, and father—how they had learned the trade, where they had traveled, what they had done—instilled in him pride in his heritage and a sense of responsibility to generations gone before, grounding him firmly in a larger whole.

Vincent grew up surrounded by the craft not only in the context of his own family but also in the larger context of his local community. First, there was the rich material culture left behind by centuries of stoneworkers in his region. As Vincent walked through the streets of his town, traveled through the countryside, or visited nearby villages, he encountered daily what folklorist Henry Glassie has called "the handmade history book of the landscape."[11] Greek and Roman ruins, medieval castles, Romanesque churches, and Renaissance villas abound, visual evidence of a legacy of stone craftsmanship going back to ancient times. In Brindisi, to the south, a Roman column carved with marble figures of the gods marks the end of the Appian Way. "There's a lot of history over there," Vincent told me.

Old forms on the land were not the only source of inspiration; there was also a vital living tradition. In Vincent's day Molfetta was filled with men who "worked the stone" or were connected with the trade in some way. There were the quarry people (*cavatori*), "the men who worked in the cave," and the stonemasons (*muratori*), "the men who built the walls." There were stone carvers (*ornatisti*), stonecutters (*scalpellini*), and sculptors (*scultori*). There were the blacksmiths (*fabri*), the men who made and continually shaped and sharpened the hundreds of tools needed to work the stone.

Stone formed a common bond, a unifying thread, a basis for social relationships and daily interaction. "In those days, there were a lot of masters over there," said Vincent. "And everyone knew each other; in each trade—stonecutters, quarrymen, carvers—they all knew each other." Indeed, Vincent found that throughout the town he was recognized and known to others in terms of the trade. "The people in the stone business, in fact most of the town, they recognize me as the grandson of Master Nicola, the son of Master Paul."

Vincent came to see that the "stonemen," as they called themselves, were held in high regard by their fellow townspeople—that his father and grandfather, as master craftsmen, were men of standing in the community, respected for their skill and knowledge. "In those days the men who work on stone, the stonemen, it was quite a respect," said Vincent. "Everybody when they see on the street the stoneman, they say hello to him, they take off their hat. It was a trade that involved not the mechanical work but involved the art. Everybody knew what kind of working man was that. Some of the old men was so proud of their work. They was so precise. And everybody call him master because he was so good, so meticulous."[12]

In Molfetta shop masters worked closely together, helping each other and exchanging labor and materials when needed. "When we don't have the right size stone, sometimes they send me to another shop for a piece of stone. We used to exchange blocks of stone," he related. "And sometimes my grandfather didn't have enough work for ten guys, so you lay off two or three guys, and they go to another shop, to Master Francis, let's say. Then, if my grandfather gets a job again, he calls Master Francis and says, 'Hey, can you send me those two guys back?' And they come back. Everyone knows each other. They go all way around from one boss to another one. . . . As it was in my grandfather's shop, it was same thing in the other shops."

A spirit of cooperation existed not only among stoneworkers in the various shops but also among the members of related trades. "They understand each other, what they had to do. It was reciprocal respect," said Vincent. "All the quarry people, when my grandfather order a stone, all he has to do was give them the measure and the quality of the stone he want, whether it was the white one or the black one, and the quarry people made sure he got it right. And when the stonecutters start to put a face on the stone and some veins show up, my grandfather says, 'Put it aside.' And the quarry people, they don't doubt my grandfather's word, they don't even come to look at the faulty stone, they just send him another one. It was reciprocal respect!"

When Vincent reflects on life and work in Molfetta, the picture that emerges is one of a close network of craftsmen sharing common needs and concerns, a work community knit together by what British historian E. P. Thompson has called an "ethos of mutuality" rooted in shared experience and long-standing pride in craft traditions.[13] It was in this atmosphere of mutuality that Vincent spent his formative years. Here he learned important notions of reciprocity, respect for good workmanship, and responsibility to family tradition. He developed an occupational identity and pride in his heritage—attitudes and feelings that have stayed with him and have influenced him throughout his working life.

"You've got to be proud," said Vincent, "because, first thing, it's your heritage. It's been transmitted from the great-grandfather to the son and grandson. So you've got to be proud of that because, what happens, it begins to get in you. It's a part of you. In my particular

Roger Morigi, age twenty, Bisuschio, Italy, 1926. (Courtesy of Louise Morigi)

Roger Morigi, age six, with his three sisters in Bisuschio, Italy, circa 1913. (Courtesy of Louise Morigi)

case, I never did anything else except stone. Working the stone is a part of my life."

Roger Morigi's beginnings in the trade were in many ways quite similar. Born in 1907, in Bisuschio, a village in the province of Lombardy in northern Italy, he grew up in the heart of a major stone district—an area that for centuries has produced scores of highly skilled master carvers rigorously trained in local workshops and proudly carrying forward the accumulated skills and knowledge of generations of artisans. Like Vincent, Roger was strongly influenced by the customs and occupational traditions of his family and his region. "A lot of us worked in stone because nearby in Viggiu and another small town, Saltrio, they had the quarries, stone quarries. And the kids, in the summer, they would go up there and work. But another reason—the father would be in the stone business, and so the child take after the father. That's what they used to do."

In Roger's time Bisuschio was a small village of about 1,500 people located in the foothills of the Italian Alps about two miles from the Swiss border and six miles north of Varese in the Italian lake country. It was the kind of town, Roger said, where "you knew everybody, you even knew the chickens, who the chickens belong to!" Most of the people in his village farmed a few acres of land. However, the "main source was stone," and the majority of men made their living working "up the mountain" in the many quarries and stone shops of the nearby stone centers of Viggiu and Saltrio. "The whole town around, everybody used to work stone. Some would be stonecutter, some carvers, all mixed up, but they all had to do with stone."

A second-generation carver, Roger grew up immersed in the craft. His father, Napoleone Morigi, was a fine ornamental carver. Born about 1865, Napoleone was an orphan who had been left at a convent in Varese when he was a newborn. Raised by a local miller, he learned to carve stone at a young age, working for local masters in Viggiu and Saltrio and traveling extensively to Switzerland, Germany, and France. "That's what everyone did," said Roger. "You could earn much more and send the money back to Italy to support your family. My father was working in Zurich, Switzerland, when he was twelve years old."

In 1890 Napoleone began to travel back and forth between Italy and the United States to work on the Library of Congress and other major building projects in Washington, D.C., and New York City. "He came over here in 1890," said Roger. "First time he went to Barre. Everybody went to Barre, Vermont, because all the Italians was up there. That's where you got your job. But then from up there, you stay there a few months and learn. Then you go here, you go there, wherever they could get a job."

A "bird of passage," as such journeymen carvers became known, Roger's father would work for extended periods of time in the United States, then travel home to Italy to see his family for a few months, and then return to the United States to work again. As labor historian

Edwin Fenton wrote in his article "Italian Immigrants in the Stoneworkers' Union," this migratory work pattern was common among Italian carvers in the late nineteenth and early twentieth centuries.

> Between 1899 and 1919, 22,838 immigrants gave their occupations at entry as stonecutters. Of these, 9,566 were Italians, and 4,346 of the Italians were from the North. Judging from the complaints of union members, large numbers of "birds of passage" had traveled back and forth across the Atlantic during the late nineteenth century to work in America during the busy summer months. With the advent of machinery and overcrowded conditions in the stonecutting trade, this movement evidently ceased.[14]

Napoleone continued to work in the United States throughout the late 1800s and early 1900s, carving architectural ornaments for buildings in New York City and Washington, D.C., as well as monuments and memorials for many of the northeastern granite centers. He eventually settled in New Haven, Connecticut, and became a U.S. citizen in 1895. "My father carved a lot of ornament, like the Library of Congress," said Roger. "He worked most of his time in New Haven, doing monument work in cemeteries, angels and figures in granite. But before he went to New Haven, he worked in building [architectural carving] in New York and Washington, just like me."

Drawn by the high wages and the abundance of stonework in America's growing granite industry, Napoleone was part of a great wave of Italian carvers who settled in the stone centers of the northeastern United States during that period. As Mary Tomasi, a writer for the Work Projects Administration, noted in her 1960 article "The Italian Story in Vermont," most of the stone carvers who settled in the granite center of Barre, Vermont, between 1899 and 1906 hailed from the northern Italian towns of Carrara and Viggiu, the quarry town where Roger and his father learned their craft. "As recently as twelve years ago," she wrote, "the people of Viggiu, Italy, sent to the city of Barre, Vermont, a marble urn filled with Italian earth. An accompanying note expressed their appreciation for the opportunities and kindnesses Barre had extended to the many Viggiu workers who were making Barre their home."[15]

The Boutwell, Milne & Varnum granite quarry in Barre, Vermont, circa 1900. Many of the stone carvers who settled in Barre at the turn of the century came from stone centers in northern Italy. (Photo by O. J. Dodge, courtesy of the Archives of Barre History, Aldrich Public Library, Barre, Vermont)

When Roger first visited Barre with his father in the late 1920s, he could hear his local dialect being spoken in the streets. "In Barre, Vermont, even today they speak my own dialect," he told me. "Years ago when I went up with my father, you didn't hear nobody speak English. You walked down the street, and you thought you was in my hometown in Italy! There were so many people up there from around my hometown. They all went to Barre, Vermont, because that's where the work was. Granite. There were a lot of people I knew there."

Perhaps Roger's most vivid image of the connection between his hometown and the granite sheds of Barre is one from childhood—indelibly imprinted on his mind—of all the men who came home to Viggiu to die. "Years ago," he said, "when my father worked in the granite shops, the dust was so thick you couldn't see the man ten feet away from you. I remember the men coming back—dying at forty or fifty years old. We used to call it the American disease. It was silicosis."

From all accounts the Italian carvers who worked in the northeastern granite and marble centers were craftsmen of exceptional skill and artistry. "These men were the elite of the industry, the carvers and letterers whose skills had been shaped for generations in the workshops of Europe," wrote Edwin Fenton.[16] "The best ones came from Italy," stated a Scottish stoneworker from Barre. "No better workmen maybe, but with more of the artist in them, more of the inspiration, like the old-time sculptors."[17] Napoleone Morigi was part of that great artistic tradition.

Roger, the youngest of four children and the only son, was greatly inspired by his father—by Napoleone's stories of his travels, by the postcards he sent home from faraway places, and by the tools he left around the house—and Roger wanted to follow in his footsteps. "What influenced me most was my father because he was a carver. And he used to have tools around the house, in the closet. So when I was a little kid, I used to fool around with this and that, and the first thing I ever did, I carved a brick with my father's tools. It was a nest. I made a nest with two eggs in it. That was the first thing with my father's tools."

Another major influence that powerfully shaped his identity and his attitudes toward his craft was what Roger called "the whole atmosphere" of the town.[18] Stone carving, he told me, was "in the air." As the dominant industry and economic mainstay of his region, stone-work touched every aspect of life in his community, forming, as folk-lorist Doris Fanelli observed of workers in the Indiana stone belt, "the basis for social interaction, economic subsistence, and cultural tradi-tions."[19] Husbands, fathers, sons, neighbors, relatives, and friends all were involved in some aspect of the trade. Stonework shaped the character of the town, affecting the thoughts and actions of each gen-eration—from the small children in school, to the young men in the workshops, to the old men on the boccie courts and in the piazzas. "Unless you left town," asserted Roger, "you worked in stone."

Most of Roger's peers were keenly interested in the craft and wanted to learn. "Over here you compete in football, baseball," Roger told me. "In my hometown we compete in carving." At the age of seven Roger began to attend drawing school in the evenings. "All the children would start real early," he said. "We used to go to night school when we were six, seven, eight years old. Every little town had a drawing school, and there's one man in town who has the ability, and he teaches the children in town how to draw. So you start from that. But the most important thing was, where we learned an awful lot, we used to go to these shops, stone shops, when we were small, eleven or twelve years old."

While still in elementary school, Roger began to apprentice dur-ing the summer at the Gussoni brothers' stone-carving shop in Viggiu. "I started when I was eleven years old," he recounted, "and I used to go up a mile and a half to walk up the mountain, and up there they used to have a quarry. And oh, there must have been twenty-five or thirty shops. And everybody had about three or four, five, six appren-tices."

The three Gussoni brothers—Pio, Cecchino, and Pietro—ran a family shop that specialized in ornamental stonework, especially mon-uments and memorials for cemeteries. It was here that Roger devoted several summers to learning to carve "ornament and flowers" out of local stone and Italian marble. When he finished elementary school, Roger followed the path of many master carvers in his region and went to Milan to continue his training at the Accademia di Belle Arti di Brera. "When I was eleven years old I went to Milan. I went to Brera in Milan, the art academy, one of the best. And I stayed there

Roger Morigi (second row, seated far left) at the Accademia di Belle Arti di Brera in Milan, Italy, circa 1925. (Courtesy of Louise Morigi)

from when I was eleven years old until I was twenty-one when I came to this country."

During his years in Milan, Roger studied at the art academy in the morning, learning to draw and to model clay. In the afternoon he continued his stone-carving apprenticeship, working in the sculpture studios of Castiglioni and Violi, learning how to carve figures with a pointing machine under the direction of the sculptors. "What I would do, I used to go to school in Brera from 8:30 to 12:30. And then from

1:30 or 2:30 to about 5:00, I used to go to the sculptor's [studio] and carve. And then in nighttime I used to go from 7:30 to 9:30 to another school, what they call the *castelle*. And that's it. That's the way I learned."

This general pattern of learning—receiving some formal artistic training in addition to serving a long apprenticeship in a carving workshop—was common among stone carvers, particularly figure carvers. Documentation of Italian carvers in Barre has revealed that many of them, like Roger, attended the Accademia di Belle Arti di Brera in Milan.[20]

For ten years Roger worked in Milan, serving a rigorous apprenticeship, studying at the art academy, and returning to Bisuschio occasionally to visit his mother, Josephine, and his three sisters. In 1927, drawn by the promise of higher wages and a desire to join his father, he immigrated to the United States. At only twenty-one he set out by himself. The memory of that momentous journey across the sea was still vivid in his mind when he recounted the story nearly sixty years later.

"[My father] sent me a letter in Italy. He explained to me what to do, and I left my old town and I land in New Haven, Connecticut, all by myself. And I couldn't speak one word of English. He told me, 'When you get to Genoa, check your trunk. When you get here to New York, you go to letter M, you open your trunk, you let the man close it up, get a red cab, put the trunk in here, take it downstairs, get a cab, go to Grand Central Station, get a one-way ticket to New Haven.' He said, 'When the man pull your ticket, the next station, you get off, it's New Haven. Get a cab'—I still remember the address, 14 Prince Street—and he said, 'I'll be here waiting for you.' And when I got there, he was waiting for me."[21]

During his first few months in the United States, Roger lived with his father and worked on various carving jobs in New Haven, attending school in the evenings to learn English. His first stone-carving job in the United States was a bas-relief marble sculpture for the war memorial in New Haven's main square. "I had this little figure to carve," Roger recalled, "you know, bas-relief, maybe an inch and a half or two. And I started to carve that, and the owner up there, he was tickled to death. He said, 'My God! Oh, what a beautiful job.'

Roger Morigi (left) and his cousin arrive in New York harbor from Genoa, Italy, in 1927. (Courtesy of Louise Morigi)

Below: Roger Morigi shortly after his arrival in the United States in 1927. As a journeyman carver, Roger worked on carving jobs up and down the East Coast during the late 1920s and 1930s. (Courtesy of Louise Morigi)

Right: The cover of the Stone Cutter's Journal, *the official organ of the Journeymen Stone Cutters Association of North America, September 1897. (Courtesy of the Laborers' Archive Museum)*

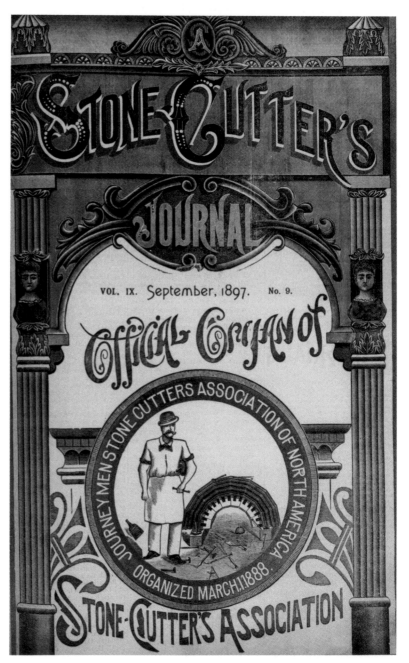

And he said to my father, 'He's doing better than you are!' My father was good. Really good. And my father says, 'He better be! He better be!' So I did the whole job. And that was the first job I did in the United States."

Shortly after his arrival in New Haven, Roger traveled to New York City to take a test to demonstrate his competence and speed as a stone carver so that he could join the union, the Journeymen Stone Cutters Association of North America.[22] His account of that experience paints a vivid picture of the carving scene in New York City in the late 1920s. Roger told the story in the context of a discussion about the great number of stone carvers from his region in Italy who were working in the northeastern United States when he started carving here in 1927. The story illustrates how immigrants identify and locate themselves in a new environment as opposed to their home terrain.

> When I went up to New York to make my sample, to take an examination, I had this interpreter because I couldn't speak English. And we came down to Saint John the Divine Cathedral because they was building it then. There was a lot of carving there, about fifty or sixty carvers working there.
>
> And there was this carver, an old man, maybe sixty years old, and he was working right there carving a crocket or something. And the president of the union, he was working there, and he came down and gave me a piece of stone, and then he brought me this model, the head of Christ, and he said, "Can you carve that?"
>
> "Sure, I can carve that." But I didn't have any tools.
>
> So he said, "Ask this guy here if you can borrow some tools."
>
> See the carvers, they're very jealous of their tools. They don't usually lend tools because they're afraid you sharpen them out of shape. So he [the carver] said, "Take what you think you need."
>
> So I took a chisel and I started roughing it out and he's watching me. And so after an hour, I'm working, he saw that I knew my business, that I knew how to carve, because you can tell right away, especially a man of his age, his experience, they can tell. Then all of a sudden I had it roughed out, you know. Then I worked a little bit more. So I did it in about two or three hours, all nice proportion and everything.

All of a sudden this guy here says to me, "Are you Italian?" He asked me in English. Well, I understood that.

"Yeah," I said. "I'm Italian."

So he started speaking Italian. And he said, "What part of Italy you come from?"

So I said, "Northern part of Italy, near Switzerland."

"Yeah? What part?"

"Milano, north of Milan."

"What city?"

"Near Varese."

"What town?"

"Bisuschio."

"Bisuschio!"

"Yeah."

"*I'm* from Bisuschio!"

Right there and then I met someone from my hometown!

Roger's story evokes the close-knit world of Italian American carvers working in New York City in the early part of the twentieth century, a golden era for Italian artisans in the United States. "When I went to the union meetings," he told me, "Oh my God! I met so many people from around my hometown. And, you know, we talk. And from there you find work. Everybody said, 'Go here,' or 'Go to the man there. He's got a lot of work.' And so we help each other."

Several months later, after joining the union, Roger returned to New York City to take a job as a journeyman stone carver for John Donnelly and Company, a large, nationally known firm of architectural sculptors and carvers. Roger's account of this experience was for him a pivotal life story—a narrative that speaks to the many challenges he faced as a young immigrant striving to surmount the barriers of language and inexperience and to establish a new life.

"It was tough," Roger said of those early days. "There was so much work, but I couldn't speak English. I can barely speak it now, but at that time I couldn't even say 'yes' in English. And they wouldn't take a chance on a twenty-one year old. My father, who also worked in this country, took me to a man [John Donnelly] I wanted to work for. But he said to my father, 'He's too young. I don't know if he knows his craft or not, and I'd hate to fire him.' At that time, in 1927, they were paying fourteen dollars a day. That was a lot of money, so a man wouldn't take a chance with a boy.

"Seven months later I went down there all by myself. I had been going to night school to learn English, and by then I could speak English better than I do now! When I went back to ask for the job, I could tell what he was thinking. Pretty soon he said, 'Weren't you in here before?' I said, 'Yes.' He said, 'But you couldn't speak English then. When did you learn?' I told him I was going to school. 'Good,' he said. And he gave me the job. I worked for him for twenty years."[23]

Thus Roger began his long career as a journeyman carver in the United States. For nearly fifteen years, throughout the Great Depression up to the beginning of World War II, he worked for John Donnelly and Company, carving figures and architectural ornament for buildings across the eastern United States. "At that time," he said, "all the building industry was going full blast. Oh my God! In New York at that time there must have been over three hundred carvers at least! There was a tremendous, tremendous amount of work."

Some of the many structures on which Roger left his mark during those years include the United States Supreme Court, the National Archives, the Department of Commerce, the U.S. Post Office, the District of Columbia courthouse, the Department of Justice, the Federal courthouse, and the Department of Agriculture in Washington, D.C.; the Bronx courthouse, Radio City Music Hall, and Riverside Church in New York City; the State Capitol of West Virginia in Charleston; and various buildings on the campuses of Carnegie-Mellon University in Pittsburgh, Yale University in New Haven, and Duke University in Durham, North Carolina.

In 1932 Roger moved to Washington, D.C., to work on the Supreme Court, for which he carved the magnificent figure of Moses for the east pediment. While in Washington, he met Louise Kavakos, the daughter of Greek immigrants, and they married in 1936. In 1941, when the United States entered World War II, John Donnelly and Company, along with stone-carving contractors across the country, closed its doors. "When the war started in 1941, when they bombed Pearl Harbor, everything stopped. Everybody went to defense," explained Roger. Unable to practice his craft, Roger went to work as a bartender for his wife's father, who owned a successful nightclub in downtown Washington. After the war, he once again picked up his tools to work on stone-carving jobs for sculptors and architects in and around Washington and New York City.

In 1956 Roger began his long and distinguished career at Washington National Cathedral, serving as the Cathedral's master carver for twenty-three years until his retirement in 1978 at the age

Master carver Roger Morigi stands beside Adam, the last sculpture he carved for Washington National Cathedral before his retirement in 1978. (Photo by Morton Broffman)

of seventy-one. It was a job he cherished above all others. "To me the Cathedral is like my home. Next to my home, it is home. When you say that, you say everything. You get attached to a place. This may be just stone to most people, but to me it's alive."[24] Roger's last carving for the Cathedral was a life-size statue of Adam for the west facade. "I finished where God began," he said of his life's work.

The significance of Roger and Vincent's backgrounds and beginnings in the trade is the extent to which stone carving was rooted in their family traditions and in their experiences of place. For both men, to be a carver was to be at the center, not at the edge, of their communities; it was to be at the locus of talk and action. The world of work did not begin and end at the stone shop door but pervaded every aspect of daily life—home, church, school, piazza, boccie courts, and streets.

Roger once told me that he learned to carve in "the traditional way." When I asked him to explain, he answered in terms of the incorporating power of tradition, painting a vivid picture of the stone-carving trade as an integral and sustaining part of daily life in his community:[25] "What I mean by that, when we started in carving, that's all we dreamed about. That was it. You always was in the atmosphere of carving. The man who taught you, he was a carver. The man who taught you at night school, he was a carver. Then you went to all these little shops and learn. Actually, you were surrounded by it, see. And even when you, when people used to go to church, there was a plaza there, and the men would stop and blab their mouths, and that's all they used to talk about—carving. What this guy here was doing, what that guy over there was doing. You see, it was the whole atmosphere! The whole thing, you were so enthused about it. You hear all the old men talk, you listen, you try to emulate. And you say, 'Oh! I want to be just as good or better.' But now there's no such thing no more. Five o'clock, you go home, goodbye, that's it."

To be a stone carver, as Roger so eloquently stated, was to belong—to be connected to one's family, friends, and neighbors and to share common bonds of knowledge, skills, values, and heritage. Stone carving bound them to the past—to a rich tradition of craftsmanship going back generations in their families and communities—and connected them to the future through the creation of a lasting legacy in stone.

2. LEARNING

When I was learning, we had great carvers, great carvers. But today they're gone. And even an apprentice, what can he learn? If he doesn't see it right there being done, the poor boy, he can't learn.

ROGER MORIGI

amily and community tradition played a key role in the recruitment and the training of traditional stone carvers, but it was in the small world of the carving workshop—in close interaction with master carvers, journeymen, and apprentices—that the carvers systematically acquired their skills and knowledge, their standards of workmanship, and their aesthetic values. "My academy was the shop," said Vincent Palumbo, "with my father and grandfather."

In Roger Morigi and Vincent's view, the importance of the workshop community as a critical context for learning and performing their craft cannot be underestimated. "The most important thing, where we learned an awful lot, we used to go to these shops when we were small—eleven, twelve years old—and there were other children there, so you compete," said Roger.

"At that time, for the apprentice, it was much easier to learn because there were many jobs, many carvers. So the apprentice, he goes

Craftsmen use old-fashioned hand drills, called violins, to craft ornamental works for the Library of Congress in 1894. Roger Morigi's father, Napoleone, would have used such a tool when he was carving at the library in the early 1890s. (Courtesy of the collections of the Library of Congress)

from one place to another, and he learned all the tricks around. He had a chance to catch what was best for him, and he come up right away. That's the way a good carver comes up," said Vincent, stressing the importance of variety, of being exposed to many different craftsmen and types of jobs.

"When I was learning," Roger told me, "we had great carvers, great carvers! But today they're gone. And even an apprentice, what can he learn? If he doesn't see it right there being done, the poor boy, he can't learn."

As the carvers' comments suggest, the skills of the trade were conveyed not by formal instruction but by "precept and example" in the workshop.[1] "You don't teach anybody to carve," stated Roger. "You give them the fundamentals of carving, like you take a hammer and a point and you hit, you take a chisel and cut. But the main thing in carving, you *steal* carving. When I say steal, you see, like you're in the shop and there are seven or eight apprentice boys. One would be a little better than the other, and you have two or three carvers working in the same place, so you watch one, you watch the other; you steal a little bit from one, you steal a little bit from the other. Then you put it all together yourself. You develop your own technique."

Surrounded by stonecutters and carvers of all ages and levels of ability, exposed to a wide range of styles and techniques, inspired by the great skill of the masters and the variety and challenge of the work, Roger and Vincent learned the craft of stone carving through a traditional process of oral transmission, observation, and imitation—through listening, watching, and doing—drawing from all that was around them in the shop, trying to "catch" what was best for them.[2]

The Workshop Community

The stone shops where Roger and Vincent learned their craft were spare, simple structures, built for the hard, dusty business of working the stone. "It was as primitive as you could possibly get," said Roger of the Gussoni brothers' shop in Viggiu. "Just a roof for working outside," said Vincent, describing his grandfather's stone shop in Molfetta.

The Palumbo family shop was located on the outskirts of town on the road to the quarry, near the old twelfth-century church of

Madonna dei Martiri. "My grandfather had his shop outside the cemetery, the wall of the cemetery. He had a little shed, a little land over there rented from the city. And that's where we were working," recalled Vincent. The shed, a small, makeshift building, was constructed of stone and terra-cotta and was open on three sides. "Most of the work for stonecutters was outside," Vincent explained. "Inside [the stone yard] was a little shed with terra-cotta tile on top. Most of them, they was open all around, just one side, and we use only when it rain."

Outside the Palumbo family stone shop in Molfetta, Italy, a young apprentice pulls the string of a violin—a hand-operated drill—for Paul Palumbo (upper right) as he carves a marble statue, circa 1930. (Courtesy of Vincent Palumbo)

Vincent estimated that the shed measured about thirty feet long by eighteen feet wide. The back wall and roof supports were loosely constructed "just one piece of stone on top of the other, no mortar, no nothing." The earthen floor was packed hard with stone chips and dust accumulated over the years. Stonecutters worked on benches made from old scraps of wood or discarded slabs of stone. An oil drum filled with wood was the only source of heat during the winter.

Vincent recalled that he and the other stoneworkers used the shed only to store their tools, to change clothes, and occasionally to work on cold, rainy days. Otherwise, he said, "it was an outside life." Out in the open air, three generations of the Palumbo family, along with several journeymen stonecutters, spent their days working the stone, the little shed behind them, the tombstones and chapels of the old cemetery in front of them beyond the cemetery wall.

Roger's description of the Gussoni brothers' stone shop in Viggiu was strikingly similar. "Over there, in a small town, they just had a piece of land, maybe forty, fifty feet wide, maybe two hundred feet long. And they had a roof on top, any old roof, galvanized steel, and open all around. There was just maybe a wall in the back. And in the wintertime it was cold, but you work; you worked just the same."

The Gussonis' shop was located behind their home on the main street of Viggiu, directly across from the piazza near the center of town. In back of the house was a "great big courtyard" entered via a large doorway that opened off the street. "Stone was piled all over the place," remembered Roger. At the far end of the courtyard was the shop—"a corrugated roof and just a couple of sticks across and some posts, and that was the shop, wide open, winter or summer." In front of the shop was a garden where one of the brothers grew tomatoes and other vegetables. Behind the shop, on the other side of a low stone wall, was a boccie court where, Roger said, "all these old people, old carvers and stonecutters, they used to go and play boccie." Near the front of the courtyard, the Gussoni brothers had a small showroom, "not too much of a place," where they displayed a few monuments and kept drawings and sketches on hand for customers.

Roger recalled that about twelve or thirteen craftsmen worked in the shop "between the three brothers, two or three journeymen, and about six or seven apprentices." He described the setting this way:

"The carvers would be on one side, the stonecutters would be on the other end, and at the end of the shop there would be the forge where we used to sharpen our own tools."

As in the Palumbos' shop, a spirit of self-sufficiency and re-sourcefulness prevailed. "We had to do with the very least," said Roger. Stone carvers and cutters made do with whatever they had on hand, building all their own equipment, working from old wooden sawhorses or giant tree stumps given to them by friends and neighbors. "Sometimes people used to cut these great big trees, and they would come around and say, 'Hey Pio, I just cut a tree down, do you need a stump?' 'Yeah, yeah!' And so they used to bring it around, and you put the stone right on top there, and it's good because it's solid; it won't move."

In these family-owned shops, relations between masters, journeymen, and apprentices were personal and close. Workers in the shop were, for the most part, family members, neighbors, and friends. They shared the same skills and working knowledge, the same customs and cultural values. As a small group of craftsmen, they were knit together by common bonds of friendship and occupational identity, by feelings of loyalty to the shop and to the traditions of craftsmanship they had inherited.[3]

Roger and Vincent often described the workshop community as a family, associating it with the positive values of intimacy and connection in family life. Reflecting on the atmosphere in his grandfather's shop, Vincent remarked, "Even the apprentices, they come when they are very young, and they never leave until they are professionals. They stay for ten, fifteen years. If the master has work, they might stay forever. You get close to each other; we eat together; in winter we put a little fire in the middle of the shop, and we sit down round the fire, and we talk. We were all friends, all together." The shop also had its share of tension and conflict, of petty squabbles and jealous rivalries. "Just like brothers and sisters, we love each other, and we fight, too," said Vincent, extending the family metaphor.

While the shop was communal in nature, it was also highly structured and disciplined. "It was more like a business," said Roger. "You went there to learn. They was strict." Working relationships were structured essentially as a hierarchy, determined largely on the basis of skill and seniority. Lines of authority were clearly drawn, and cutters and carvers were keenly aware of their status and position in the shop. "It's just like in the army," said Roger. "You're a private, then a corporal, and go up—the same thing. And just like in the army, the private does all the dirty work—well, the same thing."

It is not surprising that Vincent and Roger spoke of their training as "coming up" in the trade, for they were referring in a very real sense to the long process of working one's way up the workshop hierarchy from lowest apprentice to third- and fourth-year apprentice to journeyman, all the time progressing through a series of different roles and responsibilities, gaining in skill and status, becoming masters of their craft.

One of Vincent's favorite stories underscores the dual nature of the shop—structured and communal, formal and informal—and evokes both the hierarchical structure and the deeply felt sense of community, the shared talk and customs, that lie at the heart of the workshop experience.

Every shop, they got the funny part and the sad part, especially when you've got more than half a dozen at work, like in my shop. I remember in my shop with my grandfather when we're working, you stop and say a couple of words with the guys next to you, but we gotta watch out for the master whenever he comes. We don't want my grandfather to see us talking. So when we talk, we always look on the way my grandfather is coming, and so when we saw my grandfather, my brother-in-law says, "It's rain!" That was the password. And so we name my grandfather "rain," and everybody who saw my grandfather coming gave the alarm "rain," the secret word "rain."

So when it happen my father was coming through, we say, "It's cloudy sky!" This is true! Then they put a nickname to me because I was the family relation. So I was the "sun in the sky," the "clear air," and when they saw me, they keep on talkin'!

As Vincent's story suggests, at the top of the workshop hierarchy, in the position of ultimate authority, was the shop master. As the "man who was in command," he managed the shop and coordinated overall production: seeking business, dealing with clients, ordering and inspecting raw materials, supplying tools and equipment, delegating work, supervising the journeymen, and training apprentices. "The quality of the workmanship and the materials, every step in the manufacturing process, and all dealings outside the shop were his responsibility," historian Carl Bridenbaugh has written of the shop master's coordinative role.[4] Both Roger and Vincent stressed their masters' supervisory and troubleshooting skills. "He could smell it like a bloodhound, when something was going wrong," said Roger of Pio Gussoni. The shop master also played a key educational role, training new apprentices in the trade, passing down his traditional knowledge and skills to a new generation of craftsmen.

According to Roger and Vincent, shop masters were known for different strengths. Both Vincent's father, Paul, and Roger's master, Pietro Gussoni, were designers as well as workmen, and thus they controlled every step of the creative process from conception to execution. In addition to managing the shop, they created designs, made the drawings, sculpted clay models, produced plaster casts, and carved final works in stone. Vincent's grandfather, Nicholas, and Pietro's brothers, Pio and Cecchino, while not artistic masters, were master craftsmen in their own right, respected for their skills, their comprehensive knowledge of materials and methods, and their teaching abilities.

"Master" was a title of respect given to men of great skill. "We honor the skill of the man who earns it," said Vincent. "Even your companions, they note the difference between them and you. When they see your work, the perfection, then they start to call you 'master.'" In Roger's view, "the master is the top carver in terms of skill. You were appointed on account of your ability. You build a reputation that you was the best, and they look up to you." "Master" was also a title given to men who owned their own shops. "Whoever owns a shop is automatically a master. They give you that title because you own the shop," said Vincent. "But 99 percent who own the shop, he knows the trade."

Good masters, said Roger and Vincent, were not only skilled artisans but also creative thinkers and problem solvers who could make the most efficient and effective use of resources at hand, whether men or materials. They knew the strengths and limitations of every craftsman and carefully matched jobs with ability. They kept watch over individual growth and sought to provide their workers with enough variety and challenge to keep them happy and engaged in their work. "The talent of the foreman is to know who can do what. Then you get the best of all of them," said Roger.

Shop masters did not "retreat into the role of mere manager or isolate themselves as designers only."[5] Nicholas and Paul Palumbo and Pio, Cecchino, and Pietro Gussoni worked in their shops beside their journeymen and apprentices—carving and cutting stone, sharpening tools, setting the pointing machines, moving blocks of stone—doing whatever it took to get the job done. In later years Vincent and Roger followed the same course. "I worked real hard," said Roger of his tenure as master carver at Washington National Cathedral. "I didn't want anyone saying because you're the foreman, you're lying down. I used to do more work than all of them. I used to pull hose, put the pointing machine, and do just as much carving as they used to do sometimes."

Next to the masters in the workshop hierarchy were the journeymen carvers and cutters—fully trained professional artisans paid by the hour to produce work with speed, skill, and precision. Often they performed an informal teaching role as well, passing on the tricks of the trade to young apprentices, giving advice and suggestions drawn from their years of experience working the stone.

Roger and Vincent distinguished between three types of journeymen stoneworkers in the shops where they learned their craft: stonecutters (*scalpellini*), ornamental carvers (*ornatisti*), and figure carvers (*scultori di marmo*). Within these broad categories were artisans of varying degrees of skill. Wages and status were closely tied to ability and the type of work, with figure carvers at the top of the wage and status scale and stonecutters at the bottom. Roger made further distinctions based on what he called the "grade of work," differentiating between carvers in the "monument business," that is, commercial work, and ornamental and figure carvers who were doing "artistic" work for sculptors and architects. Carvers were evaluated according to those distinctions. Comparing the Gussoni monument shop in Viggiu with the sculpture studios where he later apprenticed in Milan, he said, "It's altogether different. When you start and learn from a man like Gussoni, it gives you inspiration because they were good; for the

Above: In large sculpture studios such as this one in Pietrasanta, Italy, circa 1923, there was often a high degree of specialization among journeymen carvers. (Courtesy of the collections of the Library of Congress)

Left: Marble carvers at work in a sculpture studio in Pietrasanta, Italy, circa 1923. (Courtesy of the collections of the Library of Congress)

grade of work they was doing, they were artists in their own right. For what they were doing, they were the best."

Although individual carvers were known and valued for their particular skills, in Roger and Vincent's experience most did not consider themselves to be specialists.[6] Vincent and his father were expert figure carvers, but they also carved all manner of ornamental work and cut tracery and moldings when necessary, combining both the artistic and the technical dimensions of their craft, maintaining control over every aspect of the trade.[7] "In Italy, in my shop, you have to be able to do everything on your own," said Vincent, "otherwise you never gonna make [it]."

Both Vincent and Roger acknowledged that in the large marble carving shops and sculpture studios in Carrara and other major stone centers there was often a high degree of specialization among journeymen carvers. "Sometimes one statue would take four carvers—one specializing in roughing out, the other in anatomy, the other in drapery, the other in hair," said Vincent. "There used to be a distinction in Carrara, in marble," recalled Roger. "One man used to carve only the faces and hands; then there was the other guy that made all the drapery; then the other guy would make only the flowers." But in the small stone shops where Roger and Vincent learned their trade, this kind of specialization usually did not exist. Rather, carvers were trained to be competent in most, if not all, aspects of their craft—prepared to handle whatever was set before them on the workbench. "They did it all," said Vincent.

Of central importance to the workings of the shop and to the continuity of the trade were the "apprentice boys." They traditionally began their training early, usually between the ages of ten and thirteen. Roger began to learn the trade at the age of ten, Vincent at the age of nine. Many of the carvers I interviewed believed that an early start and a long apprenticeship were essential to their development as professionals with a complete mastery of their craft. "Shaping stone is something that requires tremendous skill," said Constantine Seferlis, a former carver at Washington National Cathedral. "You have to get in at the right time, as a young kid. You need technical training. If they start too late, it's too hard for them . . . they stay with modeling [clay]." Roger echoed this view: "You've got to start real early and learn, and you can't have anything else on your mind, not girls, not sports, noth-ing! Just carving. If they start at eighteen or nineteen, they don't de-velop the discipline."[8]

In Roger and Vincent's experience, apprenticeships were rarely formalized with signed documents and other contractual arrange-ments. Instead, as folklorist Charles Zug observed of southern potters in the United States, a shop master "simply took on members of his family or neighbors as assistants or coworkers."[9] "Practically, there was no apprenticeship for me," Vincent told me. "I've been growing with my father and grandfather." When I asked Roger how he came to be apprenticed with the Gussoni brothers, he replied, "We knew the people personally. We grew up with them. My father knew them. So I told him [Mr. Gussoni], 'I want to learn.' And I asked him, 'Can I come up?' And he said, 'Sure, come up in the summer.'"

Drawn to the world of carving, Roger, like other boys in his hometown, had hung out around the quarries and carving shops in Viggiu, watching the carvers at work, helping out with small jobs such as polishing stone and running errands, demonstrating his com-mitment to learning the trade. It was not every boy, he told me, who had the opportunity to apprentice with the master of his choice. The great masters were known in the community, and they could afford to be selective. For prospective learners, to train with a highly respected master was to help ensure success in the trade. "It all depends on the shop you work for," said Roger. "Like over here, it depends on the university; well, it's same thing." Vincent agreed. "When you learn from a good name, you come good."

Generally carvers served an apprenticeship of between four to six years before making the transition to journeyman status. But both Roger and Vincent stressed that an apprenticeship had no predeter-mined length of time. Much depended on the ability of the individual and on shop custom. Ultimately the decision was up to the master. "When he decide you was producing something for him, then he pay you," said Roger. "Then you become a journeyman. That's the way it goes."

Vincent explained the traditional system in his community. "Over there, is no limit of apprenticeship, you see. When the younger boys start, maybe the first couple of years, they don't collect a damn

A marble quarry in Carrara, Italy, circa 1923. (Courtesy of the collections of the Library of Congress)

thing, nothing at all. Maybe at Christmas or Easter, the boss give some little thing, but they don't expect no pay, no pay at all. And then gradually, when the little boy start to produce something, then maybe the boss he start to give him so much a week. It's just completely up to the master, how much he's gonna give. There's no law. It's up to the master, if the boy he deserve, they give. And gradually, as the boy start to improve and make production, the master raise his wages, until the boy is not anymore a boy; he maybe get married, and he needs to support his family. Then they give him full pay."

In exchange for being taught a trade—a way to earn a livelihood—an apprentice worked in the shop for little or no pay. Both

Roger and Vincent, however, thought that exchange was more than fair. "You have to consider this," said Roger. "The guy who taught you, what he gives you, he gives you a gift. And if you dedicate yourself enough to learn, to make something of it, he gives you a gift that nobody can steal from you. What he give you money can't buy."

The traditional system of training was rigorous and demanding. Vincent's father and grandfather, Paul and Nicholas, and Roger's great teachers, Pio and Pietro Gussoni, were tough and exacting masters who imposed strict discipline in the shop and expected their apprentices to work hard and to show respect. "They was Christ and you was nothing!" declared Roger. "The relationship between the master and apprentice in Italy was tough. There was no fooling around. They were pretty severe. They wouldn't stop from whipping you, too."

"We listen, we obey, we learn," said Vincent of the formula for learning in his grandfather's shop. He described an episode, "one of the chapters of my training process," that illustrates the tough discipline imposed by his father.

> I had a very tough teacher—my father. I remember a lot of times my father was not an easy man. He was a sculptor, and he felt I should catch right away how he was doing. It was not easy for me. I remember one time I was carving a little capital for some columns. My father he went home for lunch—I used to eat in the shop—and me and another guy work, each one on those small capitals. And I was doing a pretty good job. It was Ionic caps.
>
> When my father came back, I don't know, for some reason I make a mistake. I make the circumference of the column the same as the cap, so my father, from about twenty, thirty feet way, when he was coming in with his bicycle, he saw the mistake I made, and he picked up the bicycle and threw it at me! He threw the damn bicycle at me! Not because I don't know—I was young, my God, maybe not even thirteen years old, and I was doing a good job—but with my calipers for some reason I make the caps too small. He was mad because I did such a good job, but then I make such an elementary mistake. Many times, many times he give me a hell of a wood shampoo!

Roger had similar experiences in the Gussoni brothers' shop. One story about a defining moment during his apprenticeship not only captures the strict, rigorous nature of his training but also speaks to the experiences that shaped his perspective and approach.[10]

I never forget one time, I got to be pretty good, so they give me a cross to carve, and the cross was like a cartouche—a cartouche is a piece of paper, rolled, you know, in stone. And there was a branch of lilies going on top. So now I'm carving this lily, and I carved it and everything fine in the front, see. Then you have to turn the cross around because you have to perforate it, you know, like the lily is sticking up free, and you have to perforate it on the other side. So I turned the cross, and when I started to perforate it, all of a sudden I heard "blumb!" I said, "Uh oh!" So I looked underneath the lily, and I'd bust the lily. I broke the lily off.

So now I get another apprentice boy, and we turn the cross around, and I'm there looking at the lily and where the lily came from, and all of a sudden here comes the boss. And this guy, they could hear him from here [Washington National Cathedral] to 14th and F [Streets] with no effort, when he talk, when he raised hell. And in back of the shop was a place where all these old people, old carvers, old stonecutters, they used to go and play boccie, you know, the game Italian boccie. And whenever they used to hear him give us hell, they all would lean on the wall and watch!

So, here he starts. I got the lily, like this, in my hands. So he takes the lily out of my hands, like that, and he stuck it underneath of my nose, and he said, "Smell it! Smell it, you dummy!" And you couldn't say nothin', you know, he was the boss. And I'm shakin' like that. And he said, "Any jackass can do that, carve it and knock it off. Smell it, you dummy!" And there were all these old men leaning and laughing like the devil. I felt like this [small].

So then he couldn't order no more, so he hit me right in the back of the neck, and he took a hammer and a tool and start— "ba-tim, ba-tum, ba-tim, ba-tum!" Knock everything off. And he just left the cartouche there and just a little piece of the branch, you know, like that. And he said, "Now take this"—the lily—"and bring it home and put it on top of the dresser, and every morning you get up, smell it good, you jackass!" And he walked away. I didn't knock anything down no more. No more! No more!

After being embarrassed in front of all the other workers in the shop and the old men on the boccie court, Roger was not likely to be careless with his work again. Such experiences impressed upon Roger and Vincent the need for constant concentration and thought, for discipline, patience, and care in a craft characterized by what David Pye has called the "workmanship of risk."[11] Indeed, both men believed that their masters' tough ways were effective methods of teaching. "His attitude made me turn my attention to my job," said Vincent of his father. "They had a certain way of teaching that would stay with you the rest of your life," said Roger. "They imprint it in your mind, the mistake you make, so next time you got to be careful not to do the same thing."

These early learning experiences not only influenced the carvers' attitudes and approach to their work but also shaped their philosophy and style of teaching. Frederick Hart, a sculptor who apprenticed with Roger at Washington National Cathedral in the early 1970s, observed that "Morigi expects to give out the same kind of training he received, and that's an attitude from another century. The master is an absolute God to the apprentice and training is rigorous. . . . You're out working early and don't put down your tools or fool around. . . . It's intensive training."[12]

The tough discipline imposed by shop masters tested the new apprentice's commitment to learning the craft, discouraging those who were not serious. "If you want to learn, you take it all," said Roger. "If you don't, you leave." But the desire to learn was not enough. Apprentices had to demonstrate an aptitude for stone carving as well. "If the master sees that you don't have the talent or ability," said Vincent, "they don't want to fool around with you." He related the story of an apprentice who was told by his father to go "fix the chairs"—a traditional saying in his hometown for someone who was "not too good."

I remember one time—this was before my days, when my father had a shop with my grandfather—my father used to take care of carving and sculpturing, and a lot of kids want to learn carving and sculpturing, and he had a bunch of them. And most of them they come pretty good, but there was this one guy who was not too good, not too bright, and my father says to him, "You know, you never gonna make [it], you better go and fix the chairs."

In my hometown it's a very low, cheap, low-down job to go around the city and yell, "Anybody want to fix the chair?" So we had this saying, when we saw someone, a mechanic or carpenter or plumber, when he's not too good, we tell him, "Hey, you better go and fix the chairs!" And my father told this kid this thing.

By God, thirty years after, in my mother's town, here comes this man around the city and yell, "Who wants to fix the chairs?" So my mother had a broken chair, and she told me to go call the guy. So I called the guy, and he start to fix, and we found out he was from Molfetta. And I was talkin' to him, and he said, "What is your name?" And I said, "Palumbo." And he said, "Are you the son of Master Paul?" I says, "Yes." And he told me, "You know, your father, he put a curse on me. Your father told me, when I was a kid and he was my master, he told me I'd better go fix the chairs!" This is true!

Thus Vincent learned lessons about maintaining excellence in the craft before he even entered the workshop. "I never forget. I still remember," he said of the incident.

Roger, too, spoke of the high expectations of the masters. He told of a young boy with whom he had apprenticed who "had the ambition but not the ability."

This boy here, his father was a butcher; his father had a butcher shop about three or four doors up from the shop where we was working in Viggiu. And he didn't like to become a butcher because all the children up there, most of us, we used to work stone, you know, because we had the quarry there. And he kind of fell in with his friends, you know, and so he wanted to learn how to carve, too. So his father said, "It's all right with me, whatever you want to do as long as you learn good." So he came down here and started to learn in Gussonis' shop.

And well, you see, in the beginning they give you a piece of rock, and then they make you make a flat surface. That's the first thing you have to learn when you're starting carving. The block is all rough, so you have to make a flat surface—straight, nice, and smooth. Of course, when you know how to carve, you might do it in an hour or two, but when you're beginning, it might take three or four days, you know what I mean. But time didn't mean anything because they wasn't paying you nothing anyway when you do that. So you gotta cut a strip on this side and a strip on this side, and then you put two strips, like a square, here, and you look to see that they're level, even. So when you get that right, whatever's in the middle you cut it all down, and then you make it even.

So that he did all right. But when he got to the middle, Mr. Gussoni came around and said, "Well, now you've got it rough like that, take an *unghiata*"—an *unghiata* is a tool like a point, but instead of four facets that come to a point, this one comes not to a point but maybe to about an eighth of an inch wide. So *unghiata.* And then *unghia,* in Italian, means fingernail. So he says, "Take the *unghiata* and pinch it." You know, what he means pinch, you take the *unghiata* and pinch it so you make all the rough stuff smaller, so after that you can take the tooth chisel and go over it, and after the tooth chisel, take the [flat] chisel.

So the poor boy, he got all mixed up. He didn't know what to do. "What am I supposed to do?" he asked. "He told me to take the *unghiata* and pinch it." So the other boys they said, "Well, you got to pinch it with your finger; *unghiata* is your little fingernail, so you pinch it." So the poor boy stood there pinching, pinching, and pinching. And the man here, Gussoni, went by and said, "What are you doing?" And [the boy] said, "Well, you told me to pinch it." And Gussoni blew his top! He told him, "Get out of here! Go back! You ain't never gonna be a carver. Go home and cut some of that meat! That you can pinch! Go be a butcher!" Man, the poor boy was so doggone mortified, but he couldn't say that we told him to do it because then he figured he'd be twice as dumb. But he wanted to be a carver.

Roger's account of the butcher boy and the *unghiata* paints a vivid picture of life and work in the shop. Embedded in his story are rich insights into the step-by-step process by which specific skills were taught—how to put a flat surface on a "rough piece of rock" and how to use new tools, like the *unghiata,* and new techniques, like "pinching" the stone. We get a sense of the master's relationship with his apprentices and gain insights into patterns of behavior among apprentices—the teasing, hazing, and traditional pranks that initiated new apprentices into the workshop community. "I'd been through all that myself," said Roger of the *unghiata* incident, "so now when someone new come by, whatever you got, you gonna give it to him. It's a chain."

The stories that carvers tell—about learning and performing, about great masters and beautiful work, about experiences on the job and customs in the shop—are significant texts. Encapsulated in these occupational narratives, whether they are tales of personal experience or stories passed down from one generation of workers to the next, are notions about correct behavior and appropriate form—attitudes, standards, and ideals that lie at the heart of who they are and what they do.[13] Such stories are important sources of information for the ethnographer because they embody, as folklorist Henry Glassie has written, "the essence of right thinking."[14]

As personal narratives, they are also rich resources for self-presentation—powerful performances of identity.[15] In telling stories about work—especially stories of apprenticeship and training—carvers locate and define themselves within the tradition. One often hears phrases such as these: "That's the way I was trained"; "that's how it was in my day"; "that's the way it used to be"; "that's the way I came up." By underscoring the kind of training they received and, by extension, their level of skill and knowledge, carvers place themselves within a certain tradition of craftsmanship and identify the sort of carvers they are.

The stone shops where Roger and Vincent learned and practiced their craft were characterized by a spirit of cooperation and competition. Working side by side, in a setting in which their skills were open to the critical scrutiny and evaluation of their peers, apprentices continually measured themselves against one another, competing for the respect and recognition accorded to skill. "There was a tremendous amount of competition," stressed Roger. "When I was growing up, like I said, there were a lot of shops, and we talk, 'Hey, this man's really good.' The voice goes around. Between ourselves we knew, we respected, the one who was doing very good, and we would say it. 'Oh, you should see the beautiful work he's doing.' And you wanted that, to hear that. And you wanted to be one of them." The rewards for mastery were social and personal, as well as economic. Carvers admired and took pride in beautiful work.

Such competition was a key motivating factor in the acquisition of skill. "It drives you to learn," said Roger. Vincent expressed it this way: "What happens, you get in love with what you're doing because it's a challenging competition between [you and] the other apprentices. You see the other guys, how they're doing, and you start to get jealous because the other boy he might be doing better than you."

Vincent's grandfather would actively push competition between apprentices in an effort to instill in them the ambition to do good work. "My grandfather was some kind of character. He try to give us the strength, not the strength, but the ambition to do good work. In those days a lot of kids want to learn how to cut the stone, and so it happened that we was five or six kids about twelve, thirteen, fourteen years old, and trying to do different things. So my grandfather came to me, and he says, 'What the hell are you doing?' He says, 'You are the master's grandson, and you do the work worse than the other kids. Take a look at that guy; he's doing faster than you and better than you.' And so he push me to do faster and better. Then he goes to the other guy and tells him the same thing. 'Look, Vincent is doing better than you. Try and beat the grandson of the master!' And he give us that ambition to do faster and good and better. So, in other words, he push competition between us, not because he want more work from us, because we were just kids that were learning, but to do better one to the other one. That was the thing. That's the way in our life we find out [how] to be a good carver, the best."

Through his grandfather's teachings, Vincent learned not only technical skills but also standards of workmanship and aesthetic principles. The good carver, he came to see, was one who placed equal value on both speed and excellence, who endeavored to produce work that was at once "faster and better."

Vincent's story points to one of the central tensions of the trade—the need to balance production and excellence. Stone carvers are first and foremost production workers. Their craft is their livelihood, a full-time occupation. For a shop owner, like Vincent's grandfather, who paid his journeymen by the hour and who was confronted daily by the economic realities of the marketplace, faster work, or as Vincent said, "making more production," meant a higher margin of profit for the shop. Thus, speed was a critical factor in workmanship.[16]

But while speed and efficiency were highly valued, so was quality. For Roger and Vincent, to produce excellent work was to reap the respect and admiration of one's peers and neighbors, to earn a good name for one's family, and to bring honor to the shop. "It was a matter of pride," said Vincent. "Your reputation goes around, especially in a small town, you see, and people, even the town, they respect you, wherever you go. You go to the butcher, and you'd be surprised, people say, 'Oh, Master Anthony, please go in front of me.' You go to the store and everybody [say], 'How you doing?' And they take off their hat. They respect you because you earn that reputation."[17]

As apprentices Roger and Vincent were taught to take pride in their work. "They wanted the best first," said Vincent. "In those days, if somebody wasn't good, they didn't hesitate to tell you to go clean the street." The best, the carvers soon learned, had as much to do with technical excellence as it did with artistic expression. Methods of instruction emphasized the perfection of technical form and the exactness of the work.[18] "The most important thing in those days was to be precise," Vincent asserted. "My grandfather used to tell me, 'What's the use of you finishing this stone in one day and then I can't use it? Spend two or three days, but we can put this stone where it's supposed to go.'"

Thus Vincent began to discover the aesthetic principles that governed the way in which work was performed and evaluated in his grandfather's shop. The good carver, he came to see, was one who produced quality work with speed, precision, and care; a craftsman who successfully balanced the need to "make more production" with the desire to do "the best first."

Masters pushed competition in the shops, encouraging apprentices to achieve individual competence, training them to become masters of their craft, but they also taught them to adhere to shared values, to temper individual creativity with responsibility to community tradition.[19] From the beginning Roger and Vincent were confronted with what folklorist Archie Green has called "the power of customary practice and expressive code on the job."[20] Through oral lore, work techniques, and shop customs, the carvers were introduced to the traditional rules that governed social interactions and the production of appropriate forms.

One of the ways in which shop rules and stylistic criteria were conveyed to apprentices was through informal rites of initiation, such as jokes, pranks, and ritualized teasing.[21] The pinching-the-stone prank is a typical example. Roger also described another joke commonly played on new apprentices in the Gussoni brothers' shop:

> Over there they had primitive things. We had to do with the very least. Like when you put a piece of stone, you just use two horses made of wood. And sometimes when somebody used to go out and go to the bathroom or something like that, they used to saw a leg, saw the piece off. So when the boy would come in and start to work, the leg would fall off, and the doggone thing would rock. And the boss would come around, and he would give the boy hell! He didn't ask who'd done it because he knew that one day or the other somebody was gonna do it.
>
> So that was part of growing up; that was part of teaching. It was a part of the life. At the same time you get to know one another better. When that is all over, then they're gonna help you. Like sometimes you're carving something, and you don't know how to do it; instead to call the boss all the time, you go to somebody in front of you that knows more than you do, and they teach you, "You do it like this."

Such ritualized forms of initiation were an integral and expected part of Roger's training as a stone carver. Ultimately these experiences were important rites of incorporation.[22] Shared by successive apprentices, they brought workers in the shop closer together, strengthening communal bonds and fostering a spirit of cooperation and a shared sense of identity and purpose.

Stone carver Constantine Seferlis's account of a common prank in the trade—sending an apprentice to sharpen a hammer—addresses themes that lie at the core of the craft: "What I remember from the old country, that is when I start systematically, I hear a lot of stories from the old people that the youngers, they have to start quite early and get into. And always they have been under harsh discipline to follow instructions and follow patterns, etcetera. And to break any ego they used to trick them. The first thing they try to introduce to him is to sharpen the hammer. They send him over and have him rubbing the hammer on the stone, and all day they laugh at him, saying, 'That is a stupid thing you are doing, but you are pleased to follow what we try to tell you because there is no room for mistakes in carving.'"

Constantine described this initiation rite as an effort by the older craftsmen to "break any ego"—to teach new apprentices that they must follow instructions and patterns. Through such customs novice carvers learned important lessons not only about respect for the authority of the masters and the ways of the shop but also about accountability—about assuming responsibility to a critical audience.[23]

As apprentices Roger and Vincent were given the latitude to develop their own styles and techniques of carving, to catch what was best for them, but they also learned that there were "limits of acceptable expression." Technical and artistic virtuosity aside, the true master operated within the boundaries of shop tradition and client expectations.[24] Ultimately the carvers understood that in the performance of their craft, as folklorist Henry Glassie has noted, what counted was not only inner competence but also the ability to relate that competence to the context that held them.[25]

The carving workshop was both a working world and a social world. United by a common purpose and shared beliefs, craftsmen worked together closely, helping one another, finding pleasure in cooperative action.[26] "In those days the collaboration was unique!" said Vincent, reflecting on the atmosphere in his grandfather's shop. "Sometimes two guys work on the same long slab of stone, but you can't beat the bush hammer at the same time or you break the stone, so they work together beating the stone one after the other, just like pistons!"

"Everybody cooperated," he continued. "One was trying to teach the other. If there was a problem with a stone, the other guys don't say, 'You make a mistake.' They were talking, almost like a committee. Four or five of the experienced men, the masters, they stand over the stone right in the middle, and everyone express his opinion. What is the best way to fix that? How can we do? It's better to cut from the bottom so the joint can be seen from the other way, or maybe we stand it up and we cut. You know, it was complete cooperation. And that include the master, the master used to ask the opinion of the people who work."

One of Vincent's favorite stories highlights the collective efforts of craftsmen to finish a piece of stone on time. Told to him by his grandfather and some of the other old-timers in the shop, the story has become for Vincent a symbol of the ethos of cooperation that characterized the nature of work and social relations in his grandfather's shop.

"My grandfather tells me once they have a job out of the town. And they have to be done at a certain time. Now the stonecutters—the day was approaching for the deadline, and they have, I think, one piece or two unfinished—so they loading the train, and the men they had to finish to cut the stone on the train. That's true! And so by the time the train reached the destination, the stone was finished! And a lot of other things like that."

Vincent's learning experiences were inextricably tied to the social dimensions of the workshop—to the comradery and fellowship, the story and song, and the shared talk and customs that were an integral part of the daily round of work. "We'd make a little fire in winter, and we'd stand around," he told me. "We used to have one hour for lunch, and the old people, I was fascinated by the old people; they would tell stories about their travels in Africa and around. And they tell the story of when they was kids, how they start. And you stand around the fire, huddled up, everybody listening. It was nice. Someone says, 'Hey, you remember that job, when we did that job, how difficult it was or how easy it was,' or 'do you remember when master so and so, he finished the stone on the train?' That's how it was, standing around, lunchtime, eating and telling stories about what happened."

For Vincent listening to the stories that the old people told about their work experiences was a major source of learning; these stories taught him the ways of the shop, introduced him to traditions of craftsmanship and codes of behavior, and gave him a sense of the criteria that governed how work was performed and evaluated.

One of Vincent's most vivid and cherished memories of working in his grandfather's shop was the singing of the stonecutters while they worked. "You know," he said, "we have a good time in my *in-fanzia* [childhood]. I remember this clear, especially when I was young and I was there trying to learn stonecutting. I remember we was about eight or nine stonecutters. We was three or four kids like me and then the old masters. As we say, all the work was done by hand. We gotta put a face on this big slab of stone with the bush hammer and things like that. And what happened, while we were working one of the guys start to sing. While he's singing, all the rest they start singing, too. And so what happened, we work by the tune of the music, of the singing. So we beat the bush hammer on the stone to make some kind of music; it was according to the singing, what we were doing. Seven, eight guys singing, you know, everybody was working, and we make more production because you can't stop, you can't split the singing. And it's many times like that."

Singing in the shop helped to set the rhythm of the work and to coordinate the men. But most of all singing made working fun: it helped to pass the time and to ease the work, generated a spirit of fellowship, and created something of beauty out of shared work experience. "It sounds incredible! It sounds incredible!" said Vincent with shining eyes and excitement in his voice. "Sometimes I remember those days, and I think, 'Well, I wish the time was just like it was before.'"

Learning to Carve

Within this context of cooperation and competition, learning to carve was characterized by a slow, step-by-step progression through a series of stages and skills. "The way they used to teach you years ago, they used to teach you very slowly, one thing at a time," said Roger. "Then all of a sudden, maybe after one and a half years, you begin to carve flowers, and you don't even know how the hell you learn to carve the flower. The teaching is so gradual." Vincent agreed. "You didn't touch a pointing machine for six years," he told me. "You had to go through the process."

The carvers' comments suggest that there was a customary way of teaching—a "process" of learning—that had been passed down over many years from one master to another. While learning the trade was not a matter of formal instruction, it was not a totally informal or unconscious process either. The complexity of the craft—the diversity of forms, materials, tools, and techniques—required both a systematic and a comprehensive approach.

Vincent described his apprenticeship as a progression through three basic stages: first, a period of watching and absorbing; then, a period of application; and finally, a period of taking responsibility for performing before a critical audience.[27] "As kids, first step you look at the other guys, what they're doing. You clean up the shop and go around and look at all the other masters and see what they doing. And little by little, as you're growing, my father started to give me a little piece of stone and make me play around. And then you get a little practice, and I started to carve. And as you're growing, your master or father or grandfather, they start to give you more responsible pieces to do. And then it's not anymore for joke; it begin to be for real. You gotta watch out what you're doing. And so, little by little, you begin to get a feel; you begin to like what you're doing."

In his grandfather's shop, Vincent began by cleaning up the shop and putting away tools, stopping whenever he could to watch the masters as they worked. He was sent on errands to deliver tools to the blacksmith and messages to the quarrymen, to buy cigarettes and drinks for the men, and to help pick up pieces of stone from neighboring shops. As he went about his chores, he was able to familiarize himself with the stone-carving process and the daily round of work.

Roger's early experiences were similar. "You clean up the shop. You do this, you do that, all the manual work. When you work, a lot of chips get on the ground, and the apprentice, the lowest apprentice, he's got to get the wheelbarrow and shovel and dump it. All that is part of it. But it's good because you learn discipline. It shows you that you have to learn, and all that makes you better, not worse."

The pattern is common among stone carvers. "You do very little carving when you first start," said former Cathedral carver Frank Zic of his apprenticeship in New York City in the early 1920s. "You had to go around and pick up the tools and sharpen the tools. You take money to pay the carvers all across the city and things like that. We had to make all kinds of things for the carvers, like scaffolds. Anything that had to be done, the apprentice boy was there to help."

One of the first jobs for the youngest apprentices was to polish stone. "It was a job for the kids," said Roger and Vincent, describing how several boys would work for hours to polish a piece of stone, rubbing it first with a block of hard stone—"a kind of granite"—and some loose black sand, and then with successively finer grades of Carborundum stone.

Another basic skill that apprentices learned early was how to sharpen their tools. Roger remembered that lesson well. "The first thing they taught me was to sharpen my tools. But the man was beside you, you see, and if you let the tool [stay] in the fire too long, it burns. And when it burns, it's no good; you have to chop it off. And every time you chop it off, you got hit on the head with his hand, 'wrum!' And I can still feel the hot flash on my neck because they didn't tap you; they hit you!"

At the Gussoni brothers' shop, Roger learned how to heat his tools in the forge, getting them red hot but not letting them burn in the fire. He then learned to shape the tools on the anvil, drawing them out to a fine cutting edge. "You shape them the way you want," he told me, "whether it was a point, a gouge, or chisel." Once he had shaped the tools to satisfaction, he learned to temper them according to the type of stone being worked.[28] "On granite," Roger explained, "the temper has to be much harder, marble softer, and limestone even softer. When you temper the tools, limestone has a little blue [color] and just a tiny bit of gold [color] at the end [at the tip of the tool as it is heated in the fire]. And marble, you've got a little blue and even more gold at the tip of the tool, but granite you've got to put in a lot of white. It's got to be real hard."

Roger's lessons at the forge and the anvil taught him about the integral relationship between tools and materials, impressing upon him that each stone had its own properties and that tools needed to be shaped and tempered accordingly. "You see, if you use the tools that you use in marble to carve limestone, it's no good because they're tempered too hard, and it's a rough cut in limestone. Instead you have to temper the tools just right for limestone, and you get a softer cut." Roger also discovered that fine work required finely sharpened tools—a simple, yet important, lesson in his craft.

Perhaps the most important task for the new apprentice was

pulling the rope for the *violino,* or violin, a hand-operated drill used by carvers before the advent of the electric drill. The violin consisted of a wooden handle and a wooden grooved spool around which a long string was wrapped. A drill bit fit into the end of the violin and was secured with a pin. While the master carver directed the violin, the apprentice pulled the string back and forth around the spool, thus spinning the drill. In the absence of an apprentice to pull the rope, carvers used a bow-shaped implement, drawing it back and forth across the spool to spin the drill, hence the name violin.

A family photograph taken outside the Palumbo stone shop in Molfetta in the early 1930s shows an apprentice pulling the string of the violin for Vincent's father as he puts the finishing touches on a statue (see page 41). An archival photograph from the Library of Congress shows craftsmen using violins and bows to carve ornamental works for the library in 1894. Roger's father, when he worked as a stone carver at the library in the early 1890s, would have used such a tool (see page 38).

It was the violin that first started Vincent working with his father in the shop at the age of nine. "At that time we didn't have an electric drill and things like that. And there used to be done a lot of tracery stuff, you know, and drapery. And we used to have a violin. And my father asked my older brother to go and pull the string of the violin, but my brother—at that time he used to work in a steel factory—he has to go to work. So I remember he comes home, and he says, 'Daddy's got a violin!' But he don't tell what kind of violin it was. So I ran to my father's shop to see the violin—the shop was about six or seven blocks distance from home—and when I get there, I get stuck! My father says, 'Come over here.' And I says to my father, 'Where is the violin?' And he says, 'This is the violin.' 'What kind of violin is that?' And my father told me, 'I'll show you what kind.' So he put the string around my hand and says, 'Pull over here.' And I started to pull the violin, and my father used to work and drill. That was the first time I start to really work."

Vincent still owns his father's old violin, a treasured keepsake imbued with memories and meaning. He has carefully preserved it and other old tools used by his father and grandfather.

In the hands of a master, the violin was an invaluable tool used to give a carving what Vincent calls "the dark"—that critical sense of depth and contrast that brings a carving to life. Vincent speaks with admiration of his father's virtuosic ability with the violin. "My father was so fantastic! With a couple of shots of the violin, he can bring out a little mouth with a different kind of expression. The violin gives the darkness to make the thing stick out. He knew precisely just where to drill the hole to make the expression."

An essential finishing tool for the master carver, the violin was also an important educational tool for the apprentice. Vincent explained: "The boy who pulls the string of the violin, he has to anticipate the turn, when the master turns, a little curve, a little thing. He has to go in front of him because if you don't turn that way, the string will come up, and the violin get stuck. And that spoils the concentration of the master. I make a few mistakes, but my father he begin to give me a little shellac [a whack], you know; he says, 'You've got to think what you're doing.' And he explain to me how to move. But still sometimes it was difficult. But after a while I learn to precede him, his movements, because I used to watch what he was doing. If he had to carve, what kind of flowers, how he has to turn, so I anticipate that fraction of a second. And I've been with him since then."

Roger also emphasized the value of the violin as a learning tool. "Oh my God! I pulled them ropes there until I was sick in the stomach! You know, but that's when you learn. I used to work for one of the finest carvers. He always wanted me to pull the rope because, you see, you gotta watch. The man has the violin in his hands; he's got the knob over here and a spool, and the rope is twisted around there. And then you pull, and the drill goes 'zzzb, zzzb, zzzb.' And you gotta watch the way the man moves, because if he moves like this, the rope has got to be straight; if he moves like that, you've gotta move over there; if it goes down there, well, you've got to follow it. And I could follow really good. And you learn an awful lot the way they used to use these drills."

Pulling the rope for the violin required Roger and Vincent to watch and to follow the master's movements carefully, anticipating his every turn. By focusing so intently on the work before them, they learned how to give the all-important chiaroscuro—the "light and dark." Although it would be several years before they reached the point of putting the finishing touches on a figure, helping their masters with the violin exposed them early in their training to the expressive dimension of their craft, to the carver's painstaking efforts to give the master touch.

As Roger and Vincent went about their many tasks—sweeping the shop, running errands, polishing stone, sharpening tools, pulling the violin—they familiarized themselves with the workings of the shop. They had a chance to watch the masters and to listen to their stories, absorbing key concepts of work and behavior. Once they had learned their way around the shop, they began to "play" with the stone, learning how to hold and to handle the basic tools—training their eyes, developing strength, and building coordination and control. "When I don't have the violin to pull," said Vincent, "my father give me a piece of stone and a point and says, 'Break this down with a point.' Most of the time I miss, and I bust my hand! That's a fact." Roger related that he was given a hammer and a point and told to reduce an old piece of stone to chips. When he finished, he was told to do it again and again, until he had achieved control over the tools in his hands.

Thus began the second stage: the long period of learning by doing and by making mistakes—developing dexterity, confidence, and control through years of practice and experience. "See my thumb? From here to here I didn't have any skin on my thumb for years! Every time you miss the chisel—wham!" exclaimed Roger, emphasizing the hands-on nature of the learning process. Other stoneworkers have described their training in similar terms. "They say that you won't be a mason until you've taken enough skin off your hands to make an apron," a master stonemason told me. "You learn from the mistakes you made before," stated Vincent.

Vincent outlined a common path of development for carvers in this second stage.

> The first thing you've got to learn [is] how to draw the letters, the alphabet, in stone. So when you learn how to draw the letters, you get a couple of tools and start carving the letters in a piece of stone. And while [I] get experience, my father started to give me a little work, let's say, put the names on some tombstones and do the inscriptions and things like that. And little by little I'm getting experience, and so I get involved like that.

But in Italy, where I come from, a good carver is gonna be able to do everything, which means before you're considered to be a stone carver you've got to be completely almost perfect as a stonecutter, which means you've got to be able to put a straight face on a slab of stone maybe two and a half meters long by a meter, meter and a half wide, with the different kinds of tools—we call a six-teeth or an eight-teeth point. Then we have a bush hammer, which has from six teeth to twenty-four teeth. And you've got to be able to put a nice straight face on the stone. Then the next step when you are good to do that thing, you start to do a cornice on stone, moldings and things like that, and so forth. And then when you're pretty good—perfect—as a stonecutter, you start to do some leaves, some ornamental things on the carving side. And so like that, little by little. And then my father start to make me use a pointing machine roughin' out work for him, like statues or relief, bas-relief.

For Roger and Vincent, learning to work the stone began with learning basic stonecutting techniques: working with straight lines and planes; learning how to put a flat surface on a rough block of stone; how to cut letters, moldings, and cornices; how to use templates, straightedges, calipers, and squares. As Roger said of his masters in Viggiu, "What they do up there, they start 'em on a flat surface. He draws a cross, and then he makes you cut in the cross, go down and make the cross square. When you're an apprentice, it's not easy. You're going along fine, then you get to the corner, and your hand is not strong; you change direction, the chisel slips, and 'wham!' You knock off the corner! You gotta know that you've got to carve against the strength—that's what you begin to learn. You begin to learn where to carve and how to do it."

As they mastered the skills of stonecutting, Roger and Vincent worked their way up, little by little, to more complicated things—learning to carve flowers, foliage, ornamental capitals, and other decorative pieces. "It depend what it was in the shop to do," Vincent said. "Gradually, if the master sees you were good at carving, he begin to give you more work in that line."

Once they had demonstrated their competence in ornamental

work, Roger and Vincent moved on to "roughing out" figures with a pointing machine. Vincent described his experience with his father. "On tombstones, after he made the model, he never work with the pointing machine; he always put the pointing machine for me [to use], to help me learn how. So I roughed out for him, and after I put the points, he come up and finished it." Vincent's carving lesson, however, did not end there; a critical part of his education was watching his father put the finishing touches on the piece. "After I point the things, that didn't mean I was free. I had to stay right there beside him and look at him. If I was looking somewhere else or doing something else—pomb! I get a little smack on the back of my head. I had to stay there and watch; that was the only way I could learn."

Roger spent years of his apprenticeship roughing out figures for his masters in Milan. "Suppose they have a figure to carve in marble. So the carver, the journeyman, he puts the main points on. Then he would tell you, 'Go ahead, put a point here, put a point there.' That's how he teaches you. He says, 'Now cut all this off.' Then he says, 'Put a point here, and now you cut all that off.' That's how you learn. He comes around, and he shows you the right line, the right plane, and perspective. But you learn an awful lot only looking at him, to see what he was doing. You see from the beginning to the finished product. And you see the process he's going through, and you get an idea how to do things."

As Roger and Vincent progressed through their apprenticeship, mastering ever more complex forms and expanding their repertoire of tools and techniques, they developed a keen knowledge of the raw materials of their trade. "While you work, while you exercise, you learn to recognize the different kinds of stones or the marbles," said Vincent. "You learn the secrets how to work better some particular kind of stone. You learn how to recognize the veins. You learn how to recognize from the sound of the stone if the stone or marble is solid or if it has some crack. All those small things you accumulate in your mind and you keep with you, so next time you remember what you're doing, and you change technique; you change how to work."

Roger put it this way: "It comes by experience. When you're young and starting, you don't know anything about a piece of stone. Then, little by little, you begin to understand the grain and everything like that—what to do first and what to do last."

Over time Roger and Vincent learned the secrets of how to "treat" various types of stone—what kinds of tools to use and how and when to use them. "Each stone has a different technique," Roger explained.

"Like limestone—it's one of the easiest stones to carve because it's compact and it's not too hard. But then when you have marble, marble is a different story altogether. The grain is already getting to be more like glass. It snaps quicker. And then there comes granite. Then you gotta use an altogether different technique. In granite you can use a point to a certain extent, but you gotta leave at least a half an inch or more. You can't go down that close for the simple reason sometimes it snaps, and it might take off more than what you want. When you get it down like that, you've got to take what they call a diamond point—it's a short tool with four points—and you cut it all down."

"If you work on marble and use a point," Roger continued, "you have to use a point in a certain way. Marble is a sensitive material. You can hit it and get a tick that penetrates three-quarters to one inch into the marble and makes a bruise inside. It penetrates in, and you see the white mark, and it doesn't look good. This happens with marble. It's very sensitive. Always you have to know the angle. Every time you hit it, the chips have to fly. You stun marble if you hit too straight. The secret is, to use the point on marble, you make it round, make the point slightly round, so you cut."

Vincent agreed. "The master says, 'Don't use this point; only use [it] when you take off six or seven inches, but then you modify it to make it softer.' These are some of the secrets that the master who knows so much can teach you."

With knowledge came speed. Roger and Vincent developed a discerning eye, a "perpetual discipline of the hand."[29] They knew where to cut; they did not get "lost." Speed is the sign of a master, Henry Glassie has written, "the perfect demonstration of control over mind and body, tools and materials."[30] Making judgments informed by experience, Roger and Vincent began to produce work quickly and efficiently, skillfully selecting their tools and ordering their actions, moving forward with confidence to recreate in stone the composition that lay before them in plaster or on paper. "Once you learn how to do good, automatically the speed comes right there," said Vincent. "You don't have no speed if you don't know what you're doing. You get lost; you don't know where to cut first. But when you know, in your mind you see what you've got to do."

In this second stage of watching and doing, learning to carve was largely a matter of imitation.[31] "You've got to steal it," said Roger, describing the acquisition of skill. "You gotta watch this, watch that, watch him, watch his brother, watch the other brother, watch the other apprentices that were ahead of us, the way they used to do it. You see one that's really good; well, you copy a little bit of this, you copy a little bit of that."

Carvers find inspiration and guidance not only in imitating great masters but also in viewing old works. Like Pueblo potters, whose designs are inspired by ancient shards, and Turkish potters, who, as Henry Glassie has written, "visit the noble old mosques to learn from the tiles of the 15th and 16th century,"[32] stone carvers turn to the carvings that adorn the churches, municipal buildings, and cemeteries of their hometowns and the distant places they travel as journeymen. "Those cemeteries, more or less, they are some kind of gallery," said Vincent. "You go in; you look around to see how the hell they did it." Irish stone carver Seamus Murphy made the same observation of the old churches and graveyards in Ireland. "They are our models," he wrote, "and very exacting they can be."[33] Roger described the sense of awe he felt as a young journeyman viewing for the first time the hand-carved granite memorials in a cemetery in Barre, Vermont. "You see the work done in granite, and you do not believe it, that it is granite! You see a bouquet of roses; you think that if you go over and blow it, they [will] move, just attached by a little stem, one to another. I don't even know how the hell they carved that! I don't know it!"

Apprentices learn by imitating, but as they become more experienced, they begin to develop a personal style. Among carvers work techniques are highly individualized. All carvers favor different tools, different ways of working, certain touches they call their own. Roger and Vincent were encouraged to find the tools and methods that worked best for them. They learned that there was not one right way but many ways to carve. "My father used to tell me, 'If it works to wipe it with your ass, do that!'" said Roger. "You find what's best for you, what's easiest for you."

The impetus to acquire a technique of one's own was both practical and personal. In technique carvers found a vehicle for individual expression—a means of putting their own stamp on their work, the imprint of their mind and hand. Thus, in Roger's view, no carver would ever want to completely copy another carver's techniques. "The master should correct you if you make any mistakes, but they should allow you to use your own techniques, what you think, what you feel about it. As a matter of fact, I don't think they wanted, I never wanted, anybody to copy. Steal some of it from me or from any other master, but never steal the whole thing. You want to develop something of your own."[34]

The ability to produce quality work with speed and consistency signaled the end of Roger and Vincent's apprenticeships and the beginning of their careers as professional carvers, but their education in the trade did not end there. "You never stop to learn," said Vincent. "Every time you do something, it's always a different subject, a different kind of stone. Always you learn something. You are never complete." When I asked Roger, when he was seventy-nine, how long he had served as an apprentice, he replied, "I worked sixty years, and I'm still learning. I'm not finished yet."

One of the most critical aspects of the stone carvers' training was the traveling they did as journeymen. Travel provided an opportunity to meet other craftsmen, to work with different materials, to learn about new tools and methods, and to pick up new tricks of the trade.[35] John Guarente, an Italian American carver who worked at Washington National Cathedral for many years, said, "As you travel, you learn a lot, and when I met Mr. Morigi, he showed me some things. He showed me two chisels, just two of 'em. And, oh my God! I could work with just those two chisels!"

As a journeyman working on jobs up and down the East Coast in the early 1930s, Roger greatly expanded his repertoire of raw materials, learning to carve granite, Indiana limestone, and a host of different marbles—Georgia, Tennessee, Vermont—that he had never encountered during his training in northern Italy. His description of carving Georgia marble for the Supreme Court illustrates the way stone carvers continually learn new methods.

The caps [Corinthian capitals] on the Supreme Court [in the inner courtyards] are Georgia marble, and there is a tremendous difference between Georgia marble and Vermont marble. Georgia marble, the grain is much wider. You've got to work it all from the inside. If you make a leaf, a Romanesque leaf, you have to do all the inside first, and then you cut the outside. Because if you cut the outside first, get the shape of the leaf, then all the points are going to fall off.

When we were carving the caps, a lot of guys didn't know [that]. Like scrolls, you had to start at the top and finish it going down. You couldn't come back no more and fool around up here [at the top]. You had to go down, all the way down. And when you were down at the end, that was it! Some of the guys didn't know that, and they used to go wild! They couldn't understand.

When you work Georgia marble, even the tools have got to be different. They gotta be stronger. Like if you have a drill, the drill when you work limestone, it can be slanted in the back, and it's all right; it's good. But when you work Georgia marble, it can't be slanted, it has to be stout, strong. Because you have to hold it there good. If it's slanted, it wobbles in your hand and you can't get a good cut.

So I got the blacksmith over here in Washington, and I told him—he was an Italian fellow, Grosso—I said, "Look, I want you to do this and that." And he said, "OK, Roger. I'll fix it the way you want." And, as a matter of fact, I had my box of tools, and every morning [when] I had to go to work, I had to run over to about three or four other carvers because they took my tools. And I used to tell them, "Well, why don't you tell the blacksmith how to fix it. He fixed it for me; he can fix it for you, too." They said, "I don't know; yours work better." Well, sure mine worked better!

When Vincent started carving at the Cathedral, he, too, was introduced to new materials and new methods. "Until I came to this country, I never used a pneumatic hammer. I never used it in Italy. I always worked by hand."

Trained to work Italian marble and the various local limestones of his region—stones, he said, that were "four times harder" than Indiana limestone—Vincent had to master completely new tools and

A young Vincent Palumbo uses a file to put the finishing touches on a carving for Washington National Cathedral, circa 1967. (Photo by Morton Broffman)

techniques, learning how to use a pneumatic hammer, wooden mallet, and rounded chisels rather than the steel hammer and straight chisels he had been accustomed to in Italy. At first it was a tough and frustrating experience. "I came over here and worked whipped cream!" he said of the dramatic difference in raw materials.

This stone, limestone, was completely strange stone. It was too soft for me. I was so confused because I used to work hard stone, marble and like that. I made quite a few mistakes, not because I didn't know what I was doing, but because the stone was completely different. I was so frustrated. Many time I go home and cry. At that time I was young—I was twenty-five years old—and it was tough for me because all the carvers over here were over sixty years old. They had a lot of experience, and they had a lot more speed than I had. And I had to compete with them.

But in the end I had the victory because maybe I was so humiliated; I concentrated much more until I came good and started to beat those old people with much more experience. And Morigi recognized that. I remember one time I was carving a big keystone for the vault of the Cathedral, and I did a good job, and Morigi he came to see what I was doing, and then he came in here in this shop, and there was working five carvers, old people— Frank Zic, Edward Ratti, Frank Zucchetti, Gino Bresciani, John Guarente. He told them, "Go and take a look how to carve. That young kid, he's doing hell of a good job. Go over and see how he's carving." He sent those old people to see my carving, a young man, the carving I was doing. That make me feel much better.

As Roger and Vincent's experiences reveal, the stone carver's education in the trade is an ongoing process. Engaged in a craft characterized by diversity, carvers are continually accumulating knowledge—encountering new materials, subjects, and styles; learning new techniques; refining old skills—striving to perfect their craft. "To think yourself already complete is the biggest mistake you can make," said Vincent, "especially in this kind of work. You never learn completely. Because every time you start a new piece, it's a new experience, it's a different subject. So you've got to put the same concentration that you put in your first piece. You're always learning. Everyday. Everyday you learn something."

3. PROCESS

The sculptor is the creator. He creates on clay. And then when they cast on plaster is the death. And the carving is the resurrection. That's the motto of our branch of the stone business.

VINCENT PALUMBO

n a small workshop at the foot of Washington National Cathedral, Vincent Palumbo works at his banker, carving a figure in limestone.[1] The afternoon sun shines through the shop's many windows, dancing on the dust-covered walls and workbenches and on the multitude of plaster models, stone carvings, and tools that fill the room. Solid and strong, Vincent leans into his work, his massive hands deftly guiding a pneumatic hammer and chisel, sending chips of stone flying. He stops now and then to blow dust off the stone and to check his progress with a pointing machine, whistling a bit of Italian opera as he works. His bushy black mustache and black curly hair, his carver's cap, and his clothes are white with stone dust—the telltale sign of a day's work.

Vincent has worked at the Cathedral for thirty-eight years, ever since immigrating to the United States from southern Italy in 1961. Indeed, except for a few months at the Shrine of the Immaculate Conception in Washington, D.C., and some stone restoration work for the White House, Vincent has spent his entire working life in the

At work in his studio at Washington National Cathedral, Vincent Palumbo carves Frederick Hart's trumeau statue of Saint Peter. (Photo by Marjorie Hunt)

A drawing of the Cathedral's south elevation by architect Philip H. Frohman. (Photo courtesy Stewart Bros. Photographers)

United States at the Cathedral. "Practically, I spent half my life at the Cathedral," he told me. "The Cathedral is part of me. This is my world, this building."

Officially known as the Cathedral Church of Saint Peter and Saint Paul, the Cathedral, a fourteenth-century English Gothic style cathedral, sits on top of Mount Saint Alban overlooking the city. The Cathedral was originally designed by architects George Frederick Bodley and Henry Vaughan, two great masters of the Gothic style, and carried forward toward completion by Philip Hubert Frohman, who served as the Cathedral's architect for fifty years.[2] Begun in 1907, Washington National Cathedral was completed and consecrated on September 29, 1990, exactly eighty-three years after the laying of the foundation stone. Over the course of nearly a century, hundreds of skilled artisans—stoneworkers, woodworkers, artists in metal and glass, and many others—built the Cathedral's great towers and flying buttresses and crafted the many gargoyles, grotesques, pinnacles, and countless other decorative details that are an integral part of Gothic design.

Above: Setting a grand finial on the Cathedral's southwest tower in 1989. (Photo by Morton Broffman)

Left: Construction of the Cathedral's choir and crypt in 1925. (Photo by National Photo; printed with permission, Washington National Cathedral)

Starting out as the "boy"—the youngest and most inexperienced carver on the Cathedral crew—Vincent worked alongside his father under the direction of master carver Roger Morigi. As Vincent became more proficient in carving Indiana limestone, he steadily gained more responsibility and stature. After Roger retired in 1978, Vincent became the Cathedral's master carver. As such, he supervised all of the stone carving for the Cathedral's west towers, training and directing a crew of up to fourteen young carvers. Today Vincent still works at the Cathedral—the only carver to remain—crafting the many stones that still need to be embellished.

How does Vincent go about his work? What are the tools, materials, and techniques that he uses to transform a block of stone into a statue—a cultural artifact? What are the specialized skills and abilities, the aesthetic attitudes, and the human values that shape and give meaning to his art? What are the standards by which good workmanship is evaluated and judged? These are the questions that guided my research as I set out to reconstruct the process of creation, striving to

Under the arches of the Cathedral's south portal, Roger Morigi uses a pointing machine to take precise measurements off the sculptor's plaster model. (Photo by Morton Broffman)

understand not only the carvers' techniques but also the ways in which they communicate shared ideas and values, personal creativity, and cultural experience through workmanship—through the expressive dimension of skill.[3]

The Work Context

At Washington National Cathedral stone carving takes place either in the carvers' workshop or on scaffolding on stones that have already been set in the building. For example, Vincent and three other carvers spent two years on scaffolding above the Cathedral's west entrance carving the Creation tympanum. "We made our shop right there," Vincent said of their temporary work space. Roger and Frank Zic worked for nearly a decade in cramped quarters above the south portal carving scores of angels, ornamental canopies, and sculptural works. "That door there is about nine or ten years of my life!" Roger said.

High up on scaffolding, Vincent Palumbo transfers measurements from a sculptor's plaster model to the stone for the tympanum in the Cathedral's Lincoln Bay. (Photo by Ellis J. Malashuk, courtesy of The Baltimore Sun*)*

*Above: The "family" of stone carvers in
their workshop at Washington National
Cathedral. Clockwise from center front:
Roger Morigi, John Guarente,
Constantine Seferlis, Frederick Hart,
Vincent Palumbo, Frank Zic, and Frank
Zucchetti. (Photo by Morton Broffman)*

*Right: Oswald Del Frate carves the
image of a Cathedral workman in stone
for the clerestory vaulting in the south
transept. (Photo by Brooks
Photographers)*

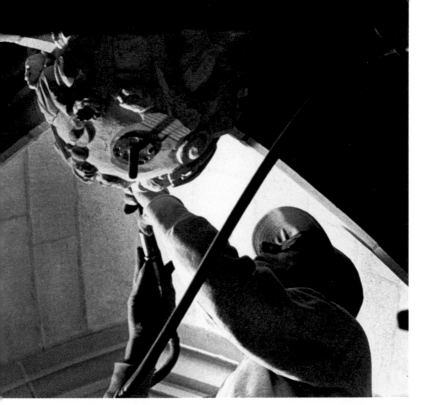

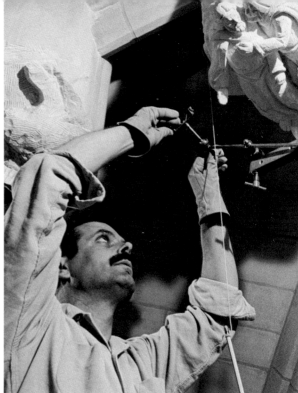

Above left: Edward Ratti carves a boss for the Cathedral's vaulted ceiling. (Photo by Robert C. Lautman)

Above right: Constantine Seferlis takes careful measurements with a pointing machine. (Photo by Morton Broffman)

Left: Frank Zic carves an angel for the south portal. (Photo by Morton Broffman)

Although a certain amount of carving takes place high on the scaffolding, the majority of work has been done in the carvers' shop. Here, over several decades, hundreds of sculptures and decorations—from freestanding statues to bas-relief carvings, from fanciful gargoyles and grotesques to intricate finials and capitals—have been handcrafted by carvers and then given to stonemasons to set in place. At one time as many as eight stone carvers worked in the shop, using their skills to interpret architects' drawings and sculptors' models.

The carvers' shop has been the key context not only for work but also for fellowship. It is here that the carvers ate their lunch, took their coffee breaks, stored their tools, changed clothes, and gathered to talk about work and to celebrate special occasions with friends and family, finding a sense of community in shared work experience and

Above: Gino Bresciani carves a cherub. (Photo by Brooks Photographers)

Right: Vincent Palumbo and John Guarente discuss their work on a large boss for the Cathedral's Churchill Bay. (Photo by Morton Broffman)

pleasure in the companionship of others. "We used to have a good time, everyone enjoying themselves," remembered Roger. "That was the beauty of it." Vincent characterized the workshop experience in terms that William Morris, a nineteenth-century English poet and artist, might have used.[4] In the workshop, life and work seemed as one. "It used to be just like a family," Vincent said. "You know, like my father, Morigi, Ratti, Bresciani, Guarente, Del Negro, Seferlis, Zic. We work and we laugh; we joke. Practically it was not work what we was doing; it was just living, everyday living!"

The workshop was also the key context for performance—a setting in which carvers assumed "accountability" to an audience for the display of technical mastery.[5] In an arena in which skills were open to the constant scrutiny and evaluation of peers, work took on a strong

The stone carvers' workshop, studio, and stone yard in 1978. (Photo by Marjorie Hunt)

Above right: The entrance to the carvers' workshop is marked by the wooden template for the Gothic canopy for the Majestus. (Photo by Marjorie Hunt)

Above left: The stone carvers' workshop stands in the shadow of Washington National Cathedral. (Photo by Marjorie Hunt)

aspect of performance, with carvers displaying their artistic competence before the ultimate critical audience—their fellow workers.

Following a centuries-old tradition, the stone carvers' shop stands in the shadow of the Cathedral, directly across from the northwest entrance.[6] Built in the early 1960s, the small wooden building, measuring twenty-seven feet five inches long by nineteen feet nine inches wide, has a low gable roof and windows on three sides. During the 1980s, when I made my observations of the workshop setting, the shop was part of a larger work area that also included the master

carver's studio, a stone yard—filled with precut blocks of stone and completed carvings—and several old masons' sheds, all surrounded by a seven-foot-high wooden fence.

The entrance to the main carving shop—a large double door-way—was framed overhead by the wooden template for an elaborate Gothic-style canopy, the sort that shields saints and angels in cathedral niches. It was the model of the canopy for the Majestus, the center-piece of the high altar reredos, carved by Roger and Frank Zic in the early 1970s. To the right of the door hung a plaster model for one of

The stone carvers' workshop at Washington National Cathedral in 1980. The carvers used to gather every work-day to eat lunch at the cloth-covered kitchen table. (Photo by Marjorie Hunt

The stone carvers' workshop at Washington National Cathedral in 1982. (Photo by L. Albee)

the Cathedral's ornamental keystones. The canopy and keystone—material evidence of the carvers' skill—symbolically marked the entrance to the shop.

Sunlight flooded the carving shop through a soft filter of stone dust. Through the many windows, carvers looked out on the Cathedral's rising west towers, and visitors to the Cathedral—their noses pressed against the windowpanes—peered in at the carvers at work. The space was open yet intimate, with a high ceiling, exposed wooden beams, and plain, unpainted plywood walls. In this place of dust and light with its great clutter of tools, templates, plaster models, and stone carvings, multiple layers of experience and meaning have accumulated over more than a quarter of a century of work. Gaston Bachelard wrote in the *Poetics of Space* that in the search for human values and meaning one can "read a room."[7] The carvers' workshop was an eloquent and deeply layered text, a rich construction of reality, yielding valuable insights into the stone carvers' world of work.

Along the walls of the shop, sturdy wooden workbenches or bankers, as they are also known in the trade, stood side by side about four feet apart. Built to the carvers' specifications out of solid four-by-four and two-by-four lumber, they were topped with blocks of limestone and half-finished carvings.[8] Overhead two large steel beams equipped with a trolley and chain ran the length of the room on either side. Carvers used that equipment to hoist heavy pieces of stone onto and off the workbenches. Rubber hoses for pneumatic hammers ran through wire hooks in the ceiling and were draped over metal stands near the workbenches. Rows of fluorescent lights augmented the natural light that filled the room.

Hanging on the plywood walls and from thick wooden support posts were hard hats and carving caps; calipers, carpenter's squares, and levels; thick ropes and chains for hoisting stone; shop drawings, architects' plans, clusters of cardboard templates, and scores of old plaster models for keystones, angels, bishops, and saints—the souvenirs of past work experience.

Makeshift wooden shelves—old boards placed on top of radiators and under windowsills—lined all four walls of the shop and were filled with stone-carving tools: wooden mallets, steel hammers, air hammers, calipers, rasps, drills, straight edges, pencils, scribers, sandpaper, Carborundum stone, and chisels of all shapes and sizes. An inventory of the contents of just the two shelves in Vincent's work area yielded a carver's cap, a pair of work glasses, an air hammer, a wooden mallet, two small blocks of Carborundum stone, a scriber, a pencil, three carpenter's squares of different sizes, a sanding block, part of a pointing machine, about fifty chisels lying flat on the shelves, and four coffee cans filled with chisels and rasps. "In carving you have so many variations of things, you need hundreds of tools," Vincent explained.

Throughout the shop, snapshots, scribbled notes, calendars, and cartoons were tacked on the plywood walls. One photocopied page, a classic example of what folklorist Alan Dundes has called "paperwork folklore," pictured several workmen doubled over in fits of hysterical laughter. Beneath each worker the carvers had written in their names—Roger, Vincent, Frank, Constantine. The caption read "You want it when?"

To the left of the main doorway hung a large map of Europe with several place names circled in pencil: Roger's birthplace, Vin-

In the workshop plaster models hang high on the walls and champagne bottles line the gables. (Photo by L. Albee)

cent's hometown, the island of Krk off the coast of Croatia where Frank Zic grew up, and Pietrasanta, the Tuscan home of Gino Bresciani, one of the old carvers—nicknamed "the cat"—who had worked at the Cathedral with Roger and Vincent in earlier days. The workshop was "just like the League of Nations," Roger told me, with carvers hailing not only from different parts of Italy but also from England, Greece, Germany, and the United States.

High in the gables, rows of dust-covered wine and champagne bottles lined several wooden beams. For over twenty years at every New Year the carvers had inscribed the label of a bottle of champagne with the date and the names of all the carvers who had worked at the Cathedral that year. Today these bottles, gathering dust, are evocative reminders of fellow workers and good times, emblems of continuity and connection with a place, an occupational community, and traditions of work.

In the far northwest corner of the shop, until the mid 1980s, there stood a kitchen table covered with a red and white checkered cloth where Roger, Vincent, and the other carvers gathered each day to eat lunch and to take coffee breaks. An assortment of old metal and wooden chairs surrounded the table, and many of them had carvers' names written on their backs. One chair had been fashioned into a throne. A fan-shaped piece of plywood was attached to the back, and a wooden bench had been placed under the legs to raise it an imposing distance off the ground. Inscribed on the back in big, black letters was the name MORIGI. Vincent related the story behind the chair.

"One time Morigi went on vacation. When he came back, we trying to find something to [make us] laugh a little bit, you know, to make a joke. So Morigi, after we eat lunch, sometimes he liked to lean back on his chair and take a snooze. So we said, 'Why don't we nail a piece of plywood to the back of his chair?' And we nail two cushions to the back. And we get this workbench, and we put the chair on top so it looked like a throne. And we have a laugh!"

In 1986 Vincent moved the lunch table and chairs to an adjoining shed to make room in the shop for an expanding crew of carvers. That shed—entered through a door in the shop's north wall—also housed Vincent's office, a changing room equipped with a sink and several lockers, and, at the far end, the twenty-horsepower electric air compressor that powered the carvers' pneumatic tools.

Across a sidewalk from the main carving shop stood the studio, traditionally the special domain of the Cathedral's master carver. Originally built for Roger, it was here that he carved many of his most important pieces, including the Majestus, the statue of the Good Shepherd, and the figure of Adam for the west portal. When Vincent became master carver in 1978, he too made the studio his workplace, reserving it for the carving of major sculptural works.

Over the entrance to the studio hung a handmade wooden sign inscribed in bold Gothic-style letters with the words "Fort Knox." Vincent told me that many years ago "John Guarente made that sign because when Morigi used to work in there, nobody was allowed to go in there. We had to knock and everything. So everyone say, 'Be careful not to go in Fort Knox!' And nobody can touch Morigi's tools. They're like gold. We can't touch. So we call it Fort Knox. And Guarente he came in early one morning with the sign, and we put it up." More than twenty years later, the studio is still called Fort Knox.

Smaller than the carvers' workshop, the studio measured nine-

Master mason Peter "Billy" Cleland directs the lowering of a huge block of limestone into Roger Morigi's studio for the carving of the Majestus. (Photo by Morton Broffman)

teen feet two inches long by eleven feet five inches wide. A large sky-light extended almost the entire width and length of the north side of the roof. "You always put a skylight facing north," explained Roger, "because you get the most uniform light." On the roof's south side, a rectangular opening allowed workmen to hoist heavy blocks of stone and completed carvings in and out of the studio with a crane.

The interior of the studio, like that of the main workshop, was

At work in his studio, Roger Morigi carves the Majestus, the centerpiece of the high altar reredos. (Photo by Morton Broffman)

filled with natural light. Wooden shelves covered with tools and plaster models lined the room; calipers, templates, ropes, and shop drawings hung from plywood walls. At the back of the studio, a padlocked door marked "Central Vault" (another joking reference to Fort Knox) led to the room where Vincent stored extra tools, pointing machines, spare parts, and some of the old steel chisels and drills that had belonged to his father and grandfather.

Gargoyles in the stone carvers' yard wait to take their places on the Cathedral. (Photo by Marjorie Hunt)

Behind the studio and the main carving shop, beneath the shade of several large trees, was the carvers' stone yard. Amid tree roots, weeds, and fallen leaves stood rows of precut blocks of stone awaiting the carvers' touch and dozens of completed carvings ready to take their places on the Cathedral. A giant steel gantry towered over the neatly stacked rows of stone. Several workbenches, some wooden boxes, a wheelbarrow, a hand truck, and various other pieces of equipment created a clutter on one side of the shop. Rising above the fence, the Cathedral's north tower and flying buttresses, adorned with saints and angels, gargoyles and pinnacles, formed a backdrop against the sky. In constant view, those carvings were for the carvers a daily source of satisfaction and pride—tangible embodiments of their craft.

The Carving Process

Stone carvers at Washington National Cathedral distinguish between two different types of carving: "working the model," in which carvers

Paying close attention to the sculptor's plaster model on his left, Roger Morigi uses an air hammer to carve the image of the Good Shepherd. (Photo by Morton Broffman)

Vincent Palumbo crafts a piece of tracery out of Indiana limestone. (Photo by Nancy Perry Fetterman)

carefully and exactly translate sculptors' plaster models into stone with the aid of pointing machines, and "freehand carving," in which carvers can work more freely from architectural blueprints and patterns or from drawings and maquettes to create imaginative gargoyles, grotesques, flowers, finials, crockets, and other ornamental carvings. Some of these decorative pieces, especially the fanciful gargoyles and grotesques, are designed by the carvers themselves, working within given boundaries of form and function.

Methods of carving vary according to the type of carving, the kind of stone being worked, and, to a great degree, the personal style of the carver, each working within the traditions of craftsmanship passed down over generations in the various shops where they learned their trade. "You learn the way in the particular shop where you are," declared Vincent. As Irish stone carver Seamus Murphy noted of the old carvers who taught him the trade, "They had a way of carving all detail, a way they had inherited, and they would not tolerate any deviation from it."[9] "Carving the stone is the least of it," said Roger, stressing the large, complex body of technical knowledge and experience that carvers bring to bear on their work. "It's what goes on top of that."

For stone carvers at the Cathedral, the carving process begins, not with an idea in the mind of a carver, but with a design created by an architect. "The drawing is the most important thing," said Roger. "The architect makes the drawing, and you've got to go by that. You're not doing it on your own. Each stone has its own design. Each stone has to fit." Vincent said, "We've got to follow the architectural blueprint. We can embellish, give more life, but we don't have the freedom to change any measurement."

The primary task of the carver, as Vincent and Roger made clear, is to understand and to carry out the intentions of the designer—whether sculptor or architect. "The workman is essentially an interpreter," observed David Pye in *The Nature and Art of Workmanship,* "and any workman's prime and overruling intention is neces-

Architect's drawing of the Cathedral's west elevation. (Photo by Stewart Bros. Photographers)

sarily to give a good interpretation of the design."[10] Roger and Vincent echoed that view. "When you work a model, you've got to pay attention to the form and get the form like the model," said Roger. "You have to put in not your idea but the idea of the sculptor. I try to understand and reproduce what is there; that's all. It didn't make any difference to me what it was; if it was upside down, but they put it like that, I'm gonna do it upside down. That's the way you like, that's the way you get!"

Stone carvers see themselves as performers, as creative individuals engaged in the skillful act of interpretation. Through their special knowledge and skills, their dexterity, judgment, and care, they transform designs on paper or in clay into lasting works in stone. Vincent put it this way: "The sculptor is the creator. He build, he create, he compose whatever he have in his mind. And the carver is the performer. Our work is to copy, to transfer in stone, what the sculptor he create in clay."

Using the analogy of music, Vincent compares stone carving to a musical performance. "In other words, it's the same thing like the composer write the music. Let's say Beethoven writes a nice symphony, and it's great, but when the musicians play, if the musicians are no good, that beautiful music is worth nothing. So that's the same thing in carving. The sculptor makes a beautiful piece, but it's up to the carver to make the work on stone look really good or to ruin the thing because he doesn't know how to carve."

As Vincent asserts, the carver plays an essential part in the creative process. A poor performance—that is, bad workmanship—can ruin a work no matter how perfect the original design. David Pye has also commented on "the analogy between workmanship and musical performance":

> The quality of the concert does not depend wholly on the score,
> and the quality of our environment does not depend on its design.
> The score and the design are merely the first of the essentials and
> they can be nullified by the performers or the workmen.[11]

Through a carver's deep understanding of raw materials, tools, and methods, through mastery of technique and a "will to excellence," the aesthetic potential of a work is realized.[12] "It's up to the carver to make the sculptor look good," said Vincent. "When it comes to carving stone, they don't know," said Roger. "They have to depend on us."

Two important factors—what folklorist Robert McCarl termed "shaping principles"—underlie the stone carvers' craft and influence the way they go about their work, affecting attitudes toward craftsmanship as well as determining skills.[13] First, stone carving is fundamentally a process of reduction, that is, the cutting away of excess material from a large mass to achieve a desired form. In contrast to sculptors or potters, who fashion works out of clay, creating forms through the successive addition of a soft, plastic material, carvers proceed by progressively reducing a hard block of stone, removing, as Giorgio Vasari wrote in his sixteenth-century treatise on technique, "all that is superfluous from the material under treatment" until they achieve "that form designed in the artist's mind."[14]

Michelangelo, in a letter written in 1549, noted the fundamental difference in technique between the sculptor who models clay *per forza di porre* (by the method of putting on) and the carver who works on stone *per forza di levare* (by taking away).[15] Vincent described the carving process in almost exactly the same terms. "The process is, the sculptor with the clay he has to create, so he put the clay on and on, and the form is getting big. What we're doing—we've got a big piece of stone, and we have to cut it off; we have to shrink it. We've got to reverse what the sculptor does. So, example, this arm is in here [he pointed from a plaster model of an arm to a block of stone]. So what I gotta do—I've got to take off the stone I don't need, and I've got to leave what is just exactly the shape of that figure over there."

Vincent speaks of working the stone as a process of revealing—of bringing into view—that which is hidden within the block of stone. "This square block, rough as it is, that statue is in here," he told me. "I've got to make it come out."[16] There is a sense on the part of the carver that while the work of the sculptor is to create—to give birth to—an image in clay, the job of the carver involves not so much an act of creation as an act of resurrection, of giving new and lasting life to an image in stone. "The sculptor is the creator," said Vincent. "He creates on clay. And then when they cast on plaster is the death. And the carving is the resurrection. That's the motto of our branch of the stone business."

The ultimate aim of the carver is to reveal, by chipping away all unwanted stone, the image that the sculptor created in clay, nothing more, nothing less. What matters is workmanship, the performance of skill. As Henry Glassie observed of Turkish potters, stone carvers seek not originality but perfection—the mastery of technique.[17] In his seminal book *Primitive Art,* anthropologist Franz Boas wrote:

> We recognize that in cases in which a perfect technique has developed, the consciousness of the artist of having mastered great difficulties, in other words the satisfaction of the virtuoso, is a source of genuine pleasure.[18]

Stone carvers share a deep "appreciation of the esthetic value of technical perfection."[19] In Vincent's eyes, the carver's act of giving life to an image through the perfection of skill and knowledge is as important and satisfying as the sculptor's act of creation. "It's different credits," he said, "but they both have the same feeling good." Carvers also value the tangible, lasting nature of their work. "We're doing the

Keystone of Christ on the Cross, carved by Paul Palumbo. (Photo by Robert C. Lautman)

finished product," said Vincent, "and it is our work, our handwork, that is gonna stay here forever. Our hands is gonna be there for thousands of years." Roger expressed it this way: "You look at something, and you say, 'I did that.' That kind of satisfaction money can't buy. That's the beauty of stone."

The second defining characteristic of stone carving—one that has to do with the nature of the raw materials, as well as the basic process—is the high degree of risk involved in the craft.[20] For a carver striving to exactly reproduce a given form in a material that is hard and unforgiving, the danger of making costly mistakes—of breaking the stone or cutting too deeply—is a constant reality.

"Stone breaks very easily if you don't know how to handle it," said Roger. "It can rest for a thousand years, but it can break in one second." As Roger and Vincent were quick to point out, once a mistake has been made, there's no second chance. "The sculptor with clay has the option to take off and put back," said Vincent; "the carver's got only one chance. It's got to be the right one. If he takes more than he's supposed to, he's ruined." Roger said, "You can't stick the stone back like clay. You cut it one time, and that's it; it's down on the floor!"

Risk shapes the carvers' approaches and attitudes to their work, requiring not only great manual dexterity but also patience and care. "It requires 100 percent concentration," said Vincent. "You've got to be patient and not overestimate the stone, because when you overestimate the stone, it comes back and bites you," said Roger.

Among carvers patience truly is a virtue. Within the trade the good carver is often described as patient, conscientious, meticulous, and precise. "A lot of carvers may be good carvers up to a point, but they don't have the patience to do it," said former Cathedral carver Frank Zic. When asked what makes a good carver, Roger replied without a moment's hesitation, "Patience above all!" For stone carvers, there is always an edge to their work, a sense of challenge and uncertainty. "It doesn't matter how good you are," said Vincent, "there's always a chance to make a mistake."

These primary shaping principles—the process of reduction and the reality of risk—are integral to the way Vincent approaches his craft. They inform his methods and techniques and influence and guide his creation of forms.

At the Cathedral the architect's measured drawings and plans specify exactly which stones are to be carved and detail their precise size, shape, and function—whether they are to be finials, gargoyles, keystones, niche sculptures, or freestanding figures. If the carving is to be a major sculpture, or, as Vincent puts it, "a serious job," the iconography is first determined by the dean of the Cathedral working in conjunction with the Cathedral's building committee and the clerk of the works. Once a theme has been decided, a sculptor is selected and commissioned to prepare a small preliminary model. If the maquette is approved by the building committee, the sculptor produces a full-scale clay model, which is then cast in plaster and given to the carvers to execute in stone.

Carvings of a more architectural nature, such as grotesques, gargoyles, capitals, and pinnacles, generally do not go before the building committee; they require only the approval of the Cathedral's dean and the clerk of the works.[21] Although some of these ornamental carvings are designed by sculptors and translated from plaster models into stone by carvers using a pointing machine, others are carved freehand based on shop drawings, templates, or maquettes. A number of these carvings, particularly gargoyles and grotesques, were actually designed by the carvers.

Most of the carving at Washington National Cathedral has been done in Indiana limestone. Over the eighty-three years that the Cathedral was under construction, a number of different quarries supplied limestone for the Cathedral. For many years much of the limestone was extracted by the Indiana Limestone Company in Bedford, Indiana, and the Independent Limestone Company in Monroe County, Indiana, both selected for the excellence and uniformity of the color and the texture of the stone. The quarried stones were then transported to a stone fabrication plant in Ellettsville, Indiana. Using shop drawings and shop tickets based on the Cathedral architect's original drawings, plant employees cut the stones to exact specifications with mechanical saws, planes, and lathes. Then the stones were shipped to the Cathedral for the carvers to embellish and the stonemasons to set in place. Today Vincent still carves sculptures for the Cathedral out of limestone quarried in Indiana.[22]

Much has changed, said Vincent and Roger, from their early days

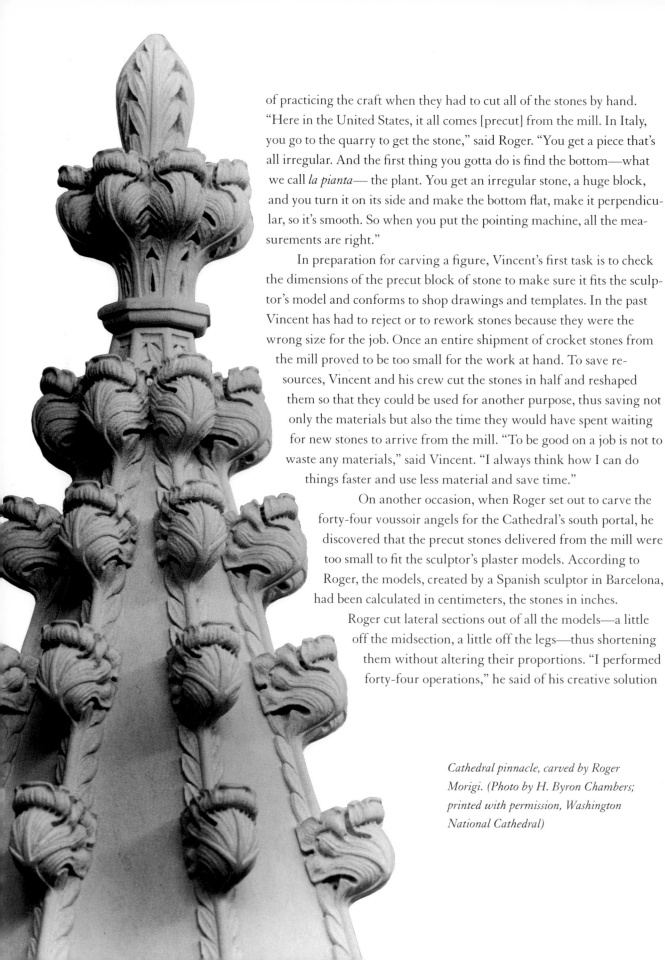

of practicing the craft when they had to cut all of the stones by hand. "Here in the United States, it all comes [precut] from the mill. In Italy, you go to the quarry to get the stone," said Roger. "You get a piece that's all irregular. And the first thing you gotta do is find the bottom—what we call *la pianta*— the plant. You get an irregular stone, a huge block, and you turn it on its side and make the bottom flat, make it perpendicular, so it's smooth. So when you put the pointing machine, all the measurements are right."

In preparation for carving a figure, Vincent's first task is to check the dimensions of the precut block of stone to make sure it fits the sculptor's model and conforms to shop drawings and templates. In the past Vincent has had to reject or to rework stones because they were the wrong size for the job. Once an entire shipment of crocket stones from the mill proved to be too small for the work at hand. To save resources, Vincent and his crew cut the stones in half and reshaped them so that they could be used for another purpose, thus saving not only the materials but also the time they would have spent waiting for new stones to arrive from the mill. "To be good on a job is not to waste any materials," said Vincent. "I always think how I can do things faster and use less material and save time."

On another occasion, when Roger set out to carve the forty-four voussoir angels for the Cathedral's south portal, he discovered that the precut stones delivered from the mill were too small to fit the sculptor's plaster models. According to Roger, the models, created by a Spanish sculptor in Barcelona, had been calculated in centimeters, the stones in inches.

Roger cut lateral sections out of all the models—a little off the midsection, a little off the legs—thus shortening them without altering their proportions. "I performed forty-four operations," he said of his creative solution

Cathedral pinnacle, carved by Roger Morigi. (Photo by H. Byron Chambers; printed with permission, Washington National Cathedral)

to the problem. "That's when we started to call him Dr. Morigi," joked Vincent.

In addition to checking the size of the stone, Vincent examines the quality of his materials to make sure there are no cracks or other serious defects. One traditional method is to tap the stone with a hammer to hear if the stone has a ringing sound. "You take a hammer and tap the block, and if it doesn't sound like a bell, then something is wrong with the block. There's a crack there, and you've got to reject the piece," said Roger, explaining the technique he used. Vincent observed, "You recognize from the sound of the stone, if the stone is solid or if it has some crack. It has to sound like a bell. From the sound, you can see if the stone, what you're doing, can come up good

Below left: Roger Morigi (on the right) and his longtime friend and associate, Frank Zic, worked together for four and a half years carving the forty-four voussoir angels for the Cathedral's south portal. (Photo by Morton Broffman)

Below right: South portal voussoir angel. (Photo by H. Byron Chambers; printed with permission, Washington National Cathedral)

work or not, because if the sound is dead, that means the stone is porous; it doesn't come too good."

A good piece of limestone, according to Roger and Vincent, has a compact grain and even texture; it should not be "crumbly" or porous or filled with fossils, pebbles, and other imperfections. For a carver, whose job is to transform raw materials into an artistic product, nothing is more discouraging than having to work a poor grade of stone. "It ruins your ambition," said Vincent, "because you work and work, and it don't come up too good."

Inferior materials deny the promise of good workmanship, making it difficult to achieve a high degree of control over technique and thwarting the craftman's best intentions and efforts. "For a carver it's very frustrating because he kills himself to do the best, and the stone won't allow it," said Vincent. Seamus Murphy echoed Vincent's strong feelings about the importance of good materials: "There are three important things to consider if you want to stay in a place: the men, the work, and the stone. If the men are good, I'm inclined to stay, if the work is interesting, I forget the men, but if the stone is bad, nothing can keep me!"[23]

Some types of stone, as Vasari noted, are "sweeter to work" than others. In Roger and Vincent's view, a piece of high-quality limestone is an excellent stone for carving. Much softer than marble or granite, it is easy to work, yet it has a compact grain that holds the cut and allows the carver to achieve sharp detail. It also is an extremely durable stone that can withstand the ravages of weather and pollution. "When limestone is taken out of the ground it contains a lot of ground water," explained Peter "Billy" Cleland, the Cathedral's master mason from 1972 to 1989. "The water helps to make it softer, but as it weathers or gets exposed to air the moisture content evaporates and it hardens. The quarrymen call this quarry sap."[24]

At the core of the carvers' working knowledge is a deep understanding of their raw materials gained over many years of firsthand experience and trial and error. Like other carvers, Vincent has strong opinions about the nature of various stones and marbles and speaks with authority about the different characteristics and qualities of each. Vermont marble is "nice," he said, because "it's like Italian marble."

Georgia marble, on the other hand, is "junk"; it "crumbles like rice." Roger agreed. "On Georgia marble some of the grain is good and tight, and some of it is open. If it's open, it crumbles; it breaks real easy. Vermont marble is much better; it's almost like Italian marble. Its only defect is it's very flaky." Pink Tennessee marble, he noted, is "sensitive"; it "resents the tools." Botticino stone is "very compact, it's just like working glass, it's sharp, it snaps like anything."

The carvers' discourse on stone illuminates not only the depth and range of their knowledge but also the deep-seated respect and emotions they have for their raw materials. When asked if he had a favorite stone, Roger replied, "I don't know if I do or not, but one stone I always did love to work—because it was so warm—was Botticino. I love to work Botticino. It's a kinda creamy color, and it's very warm. And detail, you can get detail real sharp because the stone, it's hard, hard as anything. When you work with Botticino, you have to wear gloves because the flakes are so sharp. It has very tight pores, and the slivers are very sharp. It cuts you."

Vincent said, "My favorite stone is Italian marble, Carrara white, which we call *statuario*. Not just because the giant sculptors of the past—Michelangelo, da Vinci—used it, but because it's the kind of material every little, tiny hit with a chisel brings life. And it shows immediately. Other stones, it's very difficult; it takes much more time to bring that life, to give life."

Once Vincent has checked the size and the quality of the stone he is going to carve, he hoists the block into place on a workbench in the shop using a system of ropes, pulleys, and chains. The sculptor's plaster model is placed on a workbench nearby, so that measurements can be transferred easily from the model to the stone.

Like other carvers, Vincent works standing up so that he can move freely around the stone. "We have a saying in our craft," Roger told me. "'Only the shoemaker sits down to carve.'" As they work, carvers continually adjust their position vis-à-vis the stone, moving back and forth between the model and the stone, taking measurements with the pointing machine, reaching for tools, standing on sturdy wooden boxes, and kneeling or crouching on the ground, if necessary.

"You adjust to work the stone," said Roger, telling how he had

Roger Morigi gives the master touch to a stone carving. (Photo by Morton Broffman)

learned this lesson at an early age. "When I was eight or nine years old going to nighttime school for drawing—a guy used to teach us on the easel. We'd use a box to stand on to draw, and one time I tried to move the paper to make it easier, to bring it down. And the teacher said, 'Stop! What are you doing?' And I said, 'I'm moving the paper to make it easier to work.' 'But you can't move the stone,' he said. 'What are you going to do, move the building? You have to move for the stone!'"

In the early 1980s Vincent introduced to the shop a new device he calls a rotator—a round turntable that allows the carver to spin the stone around on top of the workbench. "We have to move all the time; this way the stone comes to you," he said of his labor-saving innovation.

Vincent places the tools he has selected for the job on top of his workbench and on a tool table (sometimes simply an upturned wooden box) next to the stone. Scores of other tools lie close at hand on nearby shelves. "If you don't have tools all around you," Vincent said, "you don't feel good; you're not confident." Although stone carvers tend to surround themselves with literally hundreds of tools, they usually depend on just a few to do most of their work. "Every carver, you may have five hundred tools, but you always have those four or five tools you use all the time because they fit better in your hand; you have more confidence, and things like that," Vincent told me. Roger concurred. "Usually a carver with all the tools you got around, you only depend on a very few tools; maybe I would say a dozen, a dozen tools, no more than that, maybe even less than that. For some reason or other, [with] those dozen tools, seems like you do all kinds of work with them."

A stone carver's special tools are like old friends. The carver feels comfortable and confident with them; knows how they will behave, what they can do, the way they cut; and thus can work with maximum efficiency and effectiveness. "You'd feel lost without them," said Vincent. "Even if someone's chisel is better than yours, you don't want it." Roger added, "There are certain tools you feel confident. That's it. And you can use those tools there for most anything. It's uncanny. Sometimes you don't even believe it!" James Bambridge, the former master builder at the Cathedral Church of Saint John the Divine in New York City, expressed it this way: "You get used to your own tools, the feel of them. I think a mason would sooner leave his trousers behind than his tools!"

Stone carvers value their tools for both practical and personal reasons. Among carvers it is common for tools to be passed down from fathers to sons and from older journeymen to younger carvers coming up in the trade. Roger received numerous chisels from friends and associates over the years; many of those tools bore the names or initials of their former users inscribed on the side. Some of his tools, such as the old pointing machine that belonged to his good friend Joe

Vincent Palumbo's carving tools. (Photo by L. Albee)

Gatoni, dated back over fifty years to Roger's early days working in New York City. Vincent has many of his father's and grandfather's old steel chisels, pitching tools, and air hammers. One of his most cherished tools is a small air hammer, or *martoletto,* that had belonged to his father. "If I didn't have that little tool, I don't think I could do a thing," Vincent told me. And he added, "I keep it personally. A lot of things have sentimental value."

A stone carver's wooden mallet is especially treasured. "I wouldn't lend my mallet to anyone," said James Bambridge. "When I got my mallet, I got it from a man who had retired, and I just reshaped it to suit

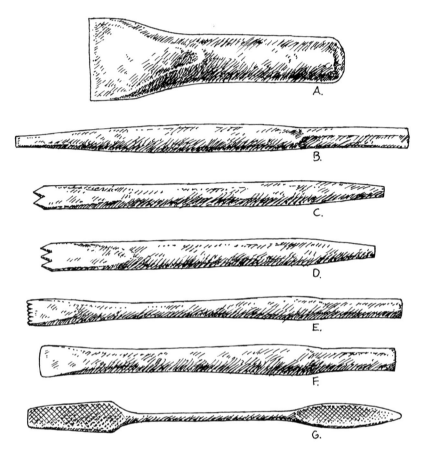

Vincent Palumbo's basic tools:
A. pitching tool, B. quarter-inch chisel,
C. two-tooth chisel, D. three-tooth chisel,
E. six-tooth chisel, F. flat chisel, and
G. file. (Drawing by Allen Carroll)

my own hand. And I have it still." Vincent still uses the mallet he bought when he first came to the United States. "The mallet I have is the one I bought back in 1964," he said. "Your mallet becomes a personal tool. You're used to that mallet, the balance, the way it fits the right way in your hand. It's part of you. If you're going to do something special, you need that mallet! You keep it like a piece of treasure."

When Roger retired, his old cherry wood mallet became a family heirloom, cherished by his wife and children. "I treasure it because I know he worked all of his life with it," said Louise Morigi. "Fifty years I worked with this mallet," Roger told me. "It's my life!"

Vincent Palumbo still uses the wooden mallet he bought in 1964 after he immigrated to the United States. (Photo by Marjorie Hunt)

Redolent with meaning, such tools have value and power beyond their practical use. "The tools of one's trade, perhaps more than any other set of objects, help to define who we are as individuals," wrote sociologists Mihalyi Csikszentimihalyi and Eugene Rochberg-Halton in *The Meaning of Things*.[25] Emblems of identity and skill, these tools embody memories of the friends, family members, or coworkers who used them and the mark they left on the world. As souvenirs of work experience, they are valued for the deep meanings and associations they hold, the vivid memories they evoke, and the link between generations they provide. Such tools not only keep alive the memories of their users but also contribute to the continuity of the craft by calling to mind attitudes and ideals—notions of right ways of working—that have been passed down over generations. When Vincent uses his father's old *martoletto,* he remembers his father's teachings and the values that were instilled in him during his apprenticeship.

With his tools, block of stone, and plaster model in place, Vincent is ready to begin carving. The first step in working the model—and, in the carvers' view, one of the most critical parts of the process—is setting the pointing machine. "You can butcher the whole block if you don't get it right!" declared Roger. "You can't miscalculate, not even one-eighth of an inch," said Vincent. "If you don't get it set right, the whole piece will be off."

The pointing machine is a mechanical device used by carvers to transfer precise measurements from a full-size model to a piece of stone. "It tells me how much stone I've got to take off," explained Vincent. "The points give me the depth of what I have to carve." While the pointing machine helps the carver determine key measurements, it does not detract from the skill and artistry of their work. "The machine only establishes the depth you have to cut," said Roger, "but from there it's up to you."

"All workmen using the workmanship of risk are constantly devising ways to limit the risk," David Pye asserted in *The Nature and Art of Workmanship*.[26] For centuries stone carvers and sculptors have used mechanical aids to limit risk and to ensure accuracy in transferring a full-size model into stone. Invented in the late nineteenth century, the pointing machine, as G. Baldwin Brown wrote in his notes to *Vasari on*

Technique, is but "the last and most elaborate" of these measuring devices. Vasari documented a painstaking method employed by sixteenth-century sculptors, such as Michelangelo, that involved using a carpenter's square to transfer the full-size model to a block of marble.

> It is necessary that against this same block, whence the figure has to be carved, there shall be placed a carpenter's square, one leg of which shall be horizontal at the foot of the figure while the other is vertical and is always at right angles with the horizontal, and so too with the straight piece above; and similarly let another square of wood or other material be adjusted to the model, by means of which the measures may be taken from the model, for instance how much the legs project forward and how much the arms. Let the artist proceed to carve out the figure from these measurements, transferring them to the marble from the model, so that measuring the marble and the model in proportion, he gradually chisels away the stone till the figure thus measured time after time, issues forth from the marble.[27]

The *Encyclopédie* of Diderot and d'Alembert, published in the mid-eighteenth century, described a system that involved placing identical wooden frames on top of both the model and the block of stone and then dropping plumb lines from which corresponding measurements could be taken.[28]

One of the most commonly used measuring devices, especially for jobs that required proportional enlargement or reduction, were calipers. "Before the pointing machine, that's the way we always used to do—to make bigger or smaller, even to copy the same size," said Roger. During Vincent's apprenticeship, he helped his father to carve figures with a pointing machine, but more frequently he used calipers, translating images into stone with what he called the "scale triangle" method, which used three different calipers to establish the position of a point in three dimensions.

Vincent described the method. "Years ago, in the old days, instead [of] a full-size model, we have, they used to call it a maquette or *bozzetto,* in Italian, and we used to do the statue from a small model, and we used to have a scale triangle. So with three calipers, different sizes, we take three measurements from the model, we scribe the triangle, and we come on stone, and we enlarge two, three, four times. It was very challenging, very difficult, very easy to make a mistake and ruin everything. But in the end [there] was more satisfaction because the work was done more with your own hands. That's how we were trained."

To set the pointing machine, Vincent first finds the center point on the plaster model, carefully measuring the width, height, and depth of the figure using rulers, tape measures, carpenter's squares, and plumb lines, if necessary. Working from these measurements, he hangs the pointing machine—which is attached to a metal armature or cross—in the center of the plaster model, making sure that the cross is plumb and level. "There's a science to putting the pointing machine," said Vincent. "Every single job is different. You have to adapt; you have to figure out what works best—how to set the machine so it fits the whole."

Next Vincent transfers these measurements to a corresponding position on the block of stone. "The hardest part is transferring the measurements to the stone," he said. "You transfer the three points to the stone, and they have to be exactly the same. The cross has to be exactly in the same spot." The process is especially complicated when it involves setting more than one pointing machine on a large sculpture. To carve the Creation tympanum on the west facade of the Cathedral, for example, Vincent had to set twenty-eight crosses on twenty-eight different sections of the plaster model. It was a job, he said, that required "imagination, common sense, and a lot of praying."

Once the pointing machine is set in place on the plaster model and the block of stone, Vincent uses a pitching tool—a heavy tool with a thick, strong, straight edge about 1½ to 2 inches wide—to "pitch off" large pieces of excess stone. Vincent's pitching tool has special sentimental value, for it is the one his father used in their family shop and brought with him to the United States over forty years ago. To use it, said Vincent, is to bring back memories of his father and the many days they spent working together.

With quick, deft strokes, a sure eye, and steady hands, Vincent hits the pitching tool with a steel hammer, sending chunks of stone crashing to the floor. "The pitching tool is a very important tool because with that you can knock off a lot of stone and rough out very fast," he said. "But you have to know how to use and when to use and where." Some carvers, Roger and Vincent pointed out, use the pitching tool more than others. "It depends on the carver, how much he trust his ability," said Roger, stressing that a good understanding of the grain of the stone is essential. "It's a good tool, but it's a very dangerous tool," cautioned Vincent. "If you don't use appropriately, you can ruin everything!" In the hands of a competent master, the pitching tool speeds up the process, removing large pieces of stone in a matter of seconds. "It gives us great relief when we have a lot of stone to work," said Vincent, "but we have to be careful."

After Vincent has pitched off the excess stone, he proceeds to rough out or "block out" the figure with a quarter-inch carbide-tipped chisel and a pneumatic hammer, starting at the top of the stone and working down, taking key measurements with the pointing machine. "You block the figure out," explained Roger. "You take the highest points all over. You block it all around until you get the main rough, what we call the 'rough' off. Then you already begin to see the shape of the figure. When you've got that, you begin to go back, and you begin to put all the individual measurements so you get the detail of the figure. You go back, easy, easy, easy. You start from the top, and you go down and get all the detail. But the first thing—the most important thing—is to get rid of all the unnecessary stone. Get rid of it! That way it gives you a better idea, in case you go a little bit deep, you see it right away. But if you have all the stone around, you don't have any idea."

Feet wide apart, Vincent leans into his work, bearing down hard and digging into the stone with the quarter-inch chisel. At this initial stage of working the "real rough stuff," he does quite a bit of carving by eye, looking from the model to the stone and using the pointing machine only to take the highest points. "Since this is just roughing out, you know you have a lot of material over here, so you can go by eye for a little while," he told me. When I commented on how quickly he went about his work, Vincent replied, "At the beginning, you worry how much you take off, but with experience you know how much will come off."

Before the widespread use of carbide tools and pneumatic hammers, Vincent, like centuries of carvers before him, would have used a hand point or *subbia*—a steel tool with four facets that come to a

With the sculptor's plaster model beside him, Vincent marks a point as he roughs out Frederick Hart's trumeau statue of Saint Paul with a quarter-inch chisel. (Photo by H. Byron Chambers; printed with permission, Washington National Cathedral)

point—to take off the "main rough." In fact, Vincent calls the quarter-inch carbide chisel a "substitute for the hand point." He uses this strong, sturdy, straight chisel when he needs to really dig in and cut down the stone. "For me it is the best chisel for roughing out. I substitute this for the hand point. Somebody else might use a different one, but for me this is the best. It does a lot of work for me."

Probably the single greatest technological change in the stone-carving process is the air hammer, which came into common use in the United States in the early 1900s, replacing the wooden mallet and steel hammer for much of the carving process.[29] Roger and Vincent only began using the pneumatic hammer when they immigrated, technological changes in the trade being slower to take hold in the small workshops where they practiced their craft in Italy. Today, like most carvers, Vincent uses an air hammer and modern carbide tools to rough out and to shape a carving in limestone, but he still relies on his traditional wooden mallet and old tempered steel chisels to put the fine details and finishing touches on each piece that he carves.

In Vincent's view, the air hammer provides a carver with a welcome power assist. "To work by hand takes a long, long time; the air compressor speeds up the work," he said, noting that a statue, which might have taken over a year to carve with a mallet, could be finished in six or seven months with an air hammer. For Vincent the air hammer is a "help to the workman's hand," increasing the speed with which a carver can work but not taking away from the carver's artistic control or skill.[30] Vincent still guides the tools, and he still relies on his dexterity and judgment. "The principle is the same," he said, comparing the air hammer to the mallet. "Inside of this machine is a piston which beat on the shank of the chisel, but you control the tools, you control the chisel."

Technological change often has its price, however, and the great disadvantage of the air hammer is the noise. The loud, steady drill of the air hammer—often many air hammers going at once—has significantly altered the workshop environment, making it a less pleasant and a far less sociable place to work. Vincent misses the rhythmic sounds of the wooden mallet and chisel hitting the stone, the singing and whistling of carvers as they work, and the sounds of nature—of birds, wind, and rain—drifting through the shop's open windows on warm days. Most of all, he misses the chance, every now and then, to engage in idle chat—to laugh and to joke—with fellow workers at neighboring workbenches.

Still for Vincent these losses are more than offset by the increase in speed and production. He especially appreciates the opportunity the air hammer gives him to move quickly through the more laborious stage of roughing out a figure, so that he can linger over the final details, lovingly adding his own personal finishing touches with a mallet and chisel. What's more, he noted, by speeding up the process the air hammer has helped to make the carver at least a little more competitive in a market-driven, profit-motivated world that places little value on quality workmanship.

At different stages of the carving process, Vincent uses air hammers of varying sizes, from large $1\frac{1}{2}$ - to 2-inch-diameter hammers for roughing out to smaller $\frac{1}{2}$ - to $\frac{1}{4}$ -inch hammers for finer work. As he works, he regulates the amount of air pressure with a valve attached to a rubber hose that runs from the air compressor to the pneumatic hammer, trying to achieve the right balance between too much air pressure and too little. As Roger pointed out, "If you don't have enough power, you scratch the stone, you don't cut." On the other hand, too much air pressure could cause the carver to cut too deeply.

Except for the fine finishing work, Vincent carves with carbide-tipped machine chisels made with a shank that fits into the end of the air hammer. Fashioned out of an extremely hard metal compound, carbide tools do not need to be tempered, and thus do not require the services of a blacksmith. Once the carbide tip has been worn down, said Vincent, the chisel is useless; "you just throw it away and buy a new one."

Both Roger and Vincent recalled earlier days, before carbide tools came into common use, when carvers relied on skilled blacksmiths—artists in metal—to temper and to sharpen their tools. "A lot of blacksmiths they were artists. They could sharpen tools so sharp they cut like a knife," said Roger. "The blacksmiths in those days they have to take a lot of credit," agreed Vincent. "There were no carbide tools in those days. They had to give temper to the tools and sharpen the way you wanted. As a matter of fact, sometimes you forget to tell the blacksmith what you're going to work, and he don't work on your tools until he send his boy, his helper, to a certain shop and a certain man, and the boy asks, 'The tools you left yesterday, what you going to do? What kind of marble you going to work? You gonna work stone or marble?'"

A good blacksmith—one who could give a lasting and perfect temper to the carver's tools—was highly prized and sought after. "My father used to say, 'When you see a blacksmith in a rocking chair, you know he's a good blacksmith,'" said Roger. He recalled how excited he was to find an excellent blacksmith when he started working in New York City in the late 1920s. "I took my whole tool box to him! He knew the temper for marble, granite, stone. They lasted forever!"

Today, however, it is difficult to find blacksmiths who have the ability to temper and to sharpen tools to a stone carver's satisfaction. Instead, Vincent has been forced to rely on carbide tools for much of his work, especially when carving marble. "In marble I'll do a lot with carbide, even finish. I finish with a hand chisel with a carbide tip. Because a regular chisel on marble doesn't work anymore because the temper is not for marble and that chisel it doesn't cut marble. So we've been forced to use carbide, and we try to find carbide very thin, very thin. But still we make do. Nothing is impossible. Today we adjust ourselves to the circumstance we have. We learn how to finish marble for the tools we have."

Vincent carefully preserves his old tempered-steel chisels and those that belonged to his father and grandfather and uses them sparingly and with the greatest care. "These are the last of the Mohicans," he said as he showed me his old tools, cradling them gently in his large hands.

Despite the introduction of the air hammer and carbide chisels, the basic methods and tools involved in carving stone have changed relatively little over the centuries. "We use the tooth chisels and points that Michelangelo used to use," stated Vincent with obvious pride in the depth and continuity of his craft. "If I go back and remember the tools my father used to use, they're the same," said Roger. "And my father, my God, if I go back, he was here in the United States in the 1890s—that's nearly a hundred years ago. They was the same tools." Indeed, the tools and processes that Vincent uses today for carving marble are virtually the same as those outlined by Vasari in the sixteenth century.

> [Sculptors] begin by roughing out the figures with a kind of tool they call "subbia," which is pointed and heavy; it is used to block out their stone in the large, and then with other tools called "calcagnuoli" which have a notch in the middle and are short, they proceed to round it, until they come to use a flat tool more slender than the calcagnuolo, which has two notches and is called "gradina": with this they go all over the figure, gently chiselling it to keep the proportion of the muscles and the folds, and treating it in such a manner that the notches or teeth of the tool give the stone a wonderful grace. This done, they remove the tooth marks with a smooth chisel, and in order to perfect the figure, wishing to add

The roughed out statue of Saint Paul shows Vincent's point marks. (Photo by Marjorie Hunt)

sweetness, softness and finish to it, they work off with curved files all traces of the gradina. They proceed in the same way with slender files and straight rasps, to complete the smoothing process.[31]

After Vincent has blocked out a figure with a quarter-inch carbide chisel and air hammer, he then uses what he calls a "rough tooth chisel," a strong, heavy-duty chisel with a deep notch in the middle of the cutting edge—what Vasari called a *calcagnuolo*. At this stage, while a lot of "fat" still is on the stone, he uses this sturdy two-tooth chisel—and later a three-tooth chisel—to remove much of the surface material, gradually going back deeper and deeper, taking frequent and meticulous measurements with the pointing machine. As he carves, he is careful always to "work the weak against the strong," for, as Roger cautioned, "when you carve something, the dangerous part you gotta do it first. You always work against the strong part, never towards the weak part. If you work towards the weak part, you break everything."

To take a measurement, Vincent first selects a point on the plaster model and works all the prominent points first, starting at the top of the stone and coming down. On any given piece, a skilled carver knows precisely where to take a measurement and when—making informed judgments based on years of experience and trial and error. In general, the greater the skill of the carver, the fewer the points that need to be taken. Trusting his eye and hand, confident of his ability, Vincent makes quick and decisive choices, carving with what to an apprentice would seem like bewildering speed. On one occasion, while observing Vincent roughing out a statue in his studio at the Cathedral, I heard the young carver assisting him marvel at how few points he had taken and how easy he made the process look. "Anything is easy if you know what you're doing," Vincent replied. "It took me forty years and many wood shampoos to learn how to do this."

Once Vincent has selected a point, he places the needle of the pointing machine in position—making sure that it is perpendicular to the surface of the model—and takes a measurement. He locks the needle in place and marks the spot on the model with a pencil. Then he carefully moves the pointing machine to the stone and takes a corresponding measurement. The needle tells him how much stone he needs to remove to reach exactly the same point on the model.

Picking up a tool from his bench, Vincent carves for a minute or two, stops to check his progress with the pointing machine, carves a little more, and then measures again. "It's a very slow motion process," he observed. Finally, "when there's maybe less than one-fourth inch,

Vincent Palumbo uses an air hammer and tooth chisel to put the finishing touches on the statue of Saint Peter. (Photo by Marjorie Hunt)

we get a little round chisel, and we drill a little hole and just leave one-sixteenth inch for when we finish with a mallet. We mark it with a pencil and leave it. That's done, that's precise." If, however, Vincent draws a circle around a point, that means that it is a "rough point" and that he still has an additional one-half to three-quarter inches of stone to remove. "If you see a circle, you know you have to do a little more,"

The nearly completed figures of Saint Peter and Saint Paul stand ready to take their places on the Cathedral's west facade. Vincent will remove the brace and finger supports after the statue of Saint Paul has been set in place. (Photo by Morton Broffman)

he said. Vincent was quick to emphasize that all carvers have their own particular systems. His father, for instance, would draw a circle around a point if he had "missed a little bit, if he went in a little bit more than he was supposed to go."

Proceeding in this way, Vincent slowly cuts away the stone "chip by chip" until eventually the figure begins to take shape in the block of stone. "We move back and forth, back and forth. We put hundreds of measurements. Then we start to connect one point to the other, and I start to clean it up." Once Vincent gets "closer to the meat," he begins to use a six-tooth chisel—a much finer, broader tooth chisel with slender, shallow teeth. Keeping a close eye on the plaster model, he goes over the entire figure, going back "finer and finer" and connecting points, using the six-tooth chisel, as Vasari wrote, to shape and refine the figure, giving "the stone a wonderful grace."

In Vincent's view the tooth chisel is an indispensable tool. "One of the most important tools in carving is the tooth chisel," he declared, although he allowed that other carvers might have a different opinion. "Each individual stone carver, they use different tools which he feels more confident. Some people—like Morigi—he didn't use a tooth chisel much. He didn't know how to use a tooth chisel because he never worked with it, so he get used to like that. But for me, and even you go back to Michelangelo, he did with a point and tooth chisel; you can see."

According to Vincent the tooth chisel can save stone carvers a great deal of time in the long run, helping them to distinguish between parts of the figure that need more work and those areas that are already finished. "The tooth chisel gives you more shadow," he explained. "After the tooth chisel, when you start to finish with the flat chisel, you can see much better the difference between the finished product and still roughing out."

Vincent's technique—a method that he learned from his father—involves leaving parts of the figure finished with the six-tooth chisel to achieve a greater sense of texture and contrast. "A lot of things need to be left with the tooth chisel," he noted. "Like when you're doing drapery or hair, even then, once and awhile, to give contrast you leave some tooth chisel marks—it gives better shadow. At least that's the way my father teach me. You learn the way in that particular shop where you are. The only studio I ever have is with my father."

Finally, after a slow and painstaking process involving hundreds of measurements, Vincent comes to what he calls the "fun part"—the final stage of carving the small details and finishing touches. "The work you are doing now is with your eye," he said. "You have to use your imagination to get the effect you want." Putting aside his pneumatic hammer and carbide chisels, Vincent turns to his wooden mallet and fine hand tools. "We use the mallet. We get a small, little chisel—we get hand chisels—and we start to do little by little, dust by dust. We start to work by hand to give all the fine movements, the small details, playing around. We try to give the movement to make look more realistic."

At this final stage, Vincent employs a variety of tools—flat chisels, curved chisels, gouges, drills, files—to achieve different effects. "That's the time when you begin to take the variation of tools," said Roger. "You gotta use all kinds of tools. You might use the drill for two minutes, then you use a gouge for ten or fifteen minutes, then you go back to the drill, to the chisel. It's according to what you have to do."

As he works, Vincent stops every five or ten minutes to sharpen his tools to a fine cutting edge on a piece of Carborundum stone. "You can't carve with dull tools, especially if you do fine work," Roger explained. "When you cut the stone, the cut is like a chew; it's not the real nice, sharp cut or soft [cut]. You can't give no color."

Probably the most critical tool at this point is a "very fresh, flat chisel." When a carver works with marble, Vincent explained, he would use files, rasps, and pumice stone to finish a carving—but not with limestone. "On limestone," Vincent declared, "you give life with a chisel." He explained.

Limestone is a very difficult material; it's a dead material. So if you file that carving [all over], it blend in everything, make uniform. It doesn't look too good. But if you finish with a chisel, you can give the effect of different colors. When you go with a chisel, if you go very soft, the stone come a little bit more dark, but if you cut a little faster, the stone under that cut, it's a little bit more white. So you give that illusion, optical illusion, to look more realistic.

If you cut faster with more pressure in the air, it comes more white. But if you do nice and soft, the stone it gets more dark, more natural color. But it's a rare, rare time when we use files on limestone [to finish all over]. It's blind. It comes only one color, no effect.

On the whole, Vincent told me, "the mark of a chisel is white; it gives a white effect." To achieve a sense of shadow and depth—what Vincent calls "the darkness"—he turns to a wide variety of gouges and drills. "When you carve with the drill, the bottom is round, it comes more dark, you get more shadow," he said. Vincent uses a gouge to "scoop out" the stone and to "give a round cut." He noted, however, that while the gouge—essentially a wood-carving tool—can be used to good effect on limestone, it is not strong enough to stand up to harder materials like marble or granite.

The drill is an especially important tool, particularly for ornamental work. Vincent uses it when he needs to go deep into small spaces, such as carving the channels around leaves, flower petals, or other botanical subjects. "If the master knows how to use the drill he can do beautiful work, more intricate," said Vincent. "He can go more deep, he can perforate more. But you've got to know where to perforate, otherwise the light goes in and you blind everything. You don't see anything."

Working skillfully with a combination of chisels, gouges, and drills, Vincent plays with the color of the stone, striving to achieve the all-important chiaroscuro, the light and dark. "When the master says, 'Give me more chiaroscuro,'" said Vincent, "that means give more power."

Most important, a good carver knows when to stop. Many carvers, Vincent noted, are good up to a point, but when they reach the stage of carving the finishing details, they go over and over the piece until it loses all sense of contrast, movement, and color. Seamus Murphy made the same observation, noting that some carvers were "well known for their ability to shape it in the block," but when it came to doing the details, they would "go over it and over it until it was dead."[32]

Vincent takes pride in his interpretive abilities—his skillful selection and use of tools, his understanding of the aesthetic potential inherent in his raw materials, his ability to give the illusion of color and movement—to give power and life—to the stone. "It's the small details that give a carving life," he said. "If you carve a rose, it's the color that makes it beautiful. When you do a rose on stone, you've got to give that exaggeration—what we call optical illusion—to make the rose, even though it's on stone, you gotta make that stone look like it's moving, make it look like real. And that's very difficult; not too many can give that touch on stone."

It is this masterful attention to detail that differentiates the great carver from the merely competent craftsman. "What makes the master is the small things," said Vincent. "That's what I call the master touch. A person who understands—the critic—when they see a figure, they look at the details. If the details has been done right, they say, 'The carver who did this, he knows what he's doing.'"

Above all, in the final details carvers leave their own personal stamp on their work—what Vincent calls his touch. The form and

Vincent Palumbo uses a file to put the finishing touches on a carving for the Cathedral's Creation tympanum. (Photo by Paul Wagner)

content of a carving may belong to the sculptor, but the surface treatment, the expressive details, belong to the carver alone. The stone carver's touch is his or her signature—a mark of individuality and, for many, a sign of the attainment of the highest degree of technical and artistic perfection. "Two, three, four, five carvers can carve the same thing," explained Roger, "but everyone of them would have a different touch, what we call a touch, you know, a certain technique that differentiates the one from the other one and the other one. It's just like you sign your own name." Vincent agreed. "And everyone can recognize his own style. Roger and I, we can recognize each other's right away, just like that!"

"That's right," said Roger. "Like the time they was carving in Baltimore, the cathedral over there, ten or fifteen years ago. And I was over there on a Saturday with my wife, and the superintendent let us in. And I went up in the scaffold, and I told him who was working in every scaffold. I told him the name of the carver. And he said, 'But you don't work here.' I said, 'I know I don't work here, but I know. Bramanti works here. Servos works there.' And he said, 'Right! How can you tell?' And I said, 'Well I can read it. That's the handwriting right there.' You see, everybody has a certain technique. If you work with them for a while, you can pick it up. Oh yeah. You can tell—very easy. Just like handwriting."

Others speak of the distinctive style of individual carvers in similar terms. Seamus Murphy wrote of his fellow Irish carvers that "they each had their own way of doing detail as individual as people's handwriting." Art historian John James has written of the medieval carvers who built Chartres Cathedral: "The same hand could be seen carving in an unvarying style over very long periods of time. . . . Though the style of the period as a whole might be evolving slowly . . . among individuals there was often no change at all."[33]

In addition to a personal style or touch, Roger and Vincent were quick to stress that within the basic progression of tools and steps of the process each carver has an individual technique of working the stone. "All carvers have a different way to work," said Roger, "and they have different tools they favor. You yourself, you have to decide what kind of tools you'll use for a certain thing. Another guy wouldn't

Roger Morigi gives the master touch to a carving with his wooden mallet and chisel. (Photo by Morton Broffman)

use the same tools." Work technique, along with personal style, is a primary vehicle for personal expression.

An exchange between Roger and former Cathedral carver Frank Zic points to the distinctive touch of the carver and highlights the ways in which carvers continually watch, evaluate, and learn from each other's work technique.

"Technique is different one man to another," Roger said.

"In the end, I don't think there's any one carver that does the same as another carver," agreed Frank.

"Right," said Roger.

"They're all different," said Frank.

"All different."

"They all have a different style completely. Completely different style."

"Right," said Roger. "Like the time when we were carving the grotesques for the Rockefeller church [the Riverside Church] on Riverside Drive—you know, the grotesques that went up on top of the door there, all the way up. And for some reason or another, the way he was touching it, his they came out like that. 'Grrrh.' Wild, full of life! And mine, eh, they was all right, but they didn't have the life. I couldn't understand how the hell he does it."

"Who was doing this?" Frank asked.

"Scafaro."

"The one with chewing tobacco?"

"Yeah, one of the great carvers," said Roger. "You know, he used to come to work with eight or ten tools. If you took one tool, he had to go home because he couldn't work. So I watch him, and I see the tools he used to give a certain touch. And he went to the bathroom, and I went over and got the tools there, and I went over and touch mine like that, and that was it! And it was all broke up tools; I wouldn't use it, you know, I wouldn't use it to work, but they was the right tools for the certain thing.

"So, when he come back, he's looking all over, he's looking all over. And I forgot about that I took his tools. So when I saw him looking all over, I said, 'Oh, doggone it, Roger, you took his tools. Now he's looking for you.' So I went back like that, and I presented them to him. I said, 'Mr. Scafaro'—because at that time then, older carvers, you call them mister—I said, 'Mr. Scafaro, is that what you're looking for?' And he could speak English perfect. You never thought he was Italian. You thought that he went to Oxford to learn to speak English, that's how perfect he used to speak. And he said, 'Yes.' And I explained why I took them. And he said, 'It makes my heart feel so good.' And I said, 'Why? I took your tools.' And he said, 'No, because you're so interested to see to make good work.' He said, 'Today, very few feel that way.' He said, 'To me, it make me feel good.'"

In Roger's story we see the emphasis that carvers place on ways of working the stone. We learn about the importance of knowing the right tools for the job and having the ability to use them effectively. We see the respect given to old masters and to efforts to strive for excellence. Above all, Roger's story underscores the aesthetic criteria by which carvers evaluate each other's work. The great carver, as Roger said, is one who can give life to the stone.

This aesthetic of realism—of striving to imitate reality and to give life to the stone—is beautifully illustrated by a traditional story, common among stone carvers, of a carver who pretends to have a terrible time carving flowers because they look so real that the bees land on them. Often told as a personal experience narrative, the story has numerous variants. John Guarente, a former Washington National Cathedral carver, told this version.

> I was carving one time a statue of Saint Joseph. Well, Saint Joseph has a stick or a branch, and the lily popped out of it, you know. So I was carving this statue, and the lily—I couldn't carve lilies very good, I wasn't much of flower carver. Well, I was carving it, and I saw this dealer. He was a dealer, a monument dealer, but he was a great carver for flowers. His name was Fabrizio.
>
> I saw Mr. Fabrizio out of the corner of my eye—he was watching me, and I was carving this lily—so I took my cap off, and I started swinging it in the air, and he said, "What's the matter, Johnny?" I says, "You know, I have such a hard time carving flowers. The bees come around. My flowers are so real"—I was kidding—"my flowers are so real, the bees come for the honey. They think it's a real flower." And he laughed at that.
>
> Well, after I come to Washington here, he died. He had finished a big monument, and it had a spray of roses on one side he had finished, but this side he had only roughed it out. So his son said, "Johnny, my daddy died. Can you come and finish that spray of roses because this monument has to go out?" Oh, it was a big, fancy monument. So I says, "All right." And so I went up there, and I carved that. I looked at his flowers—there's no

pointing machine or anything—just looking at it and carving the other spray of roses. Well, I had it all finished, and I went in the office and called his son, Romeo, and I said, "Romeo, come on out and take a look at it. I've finished the carving on that. See if there's anything that you want me to touch up a little bit." So he came out, and we're both looking at it. And do you know a bee came and went right to that rose!

Vincent told Roger and Frank Zic a similar tale about a time when he and two other carvers were working on the scaffolding at Washington National Cathedral. "It was Constantine, Malcolm, and myself. You remember? We was carving those boss on the baptistery over there, and I was carving the flowers. I finished the flowers, and all of a sudden—I was on the scaffold—I started going 'bam, bam, boom, bam!' [He waved his arms wildly.] Constantine said, 'What happened Vince? What happened?' I said, 'The damn bees have come on my flowers!' You remember? Constantine says, 'Damn, Vincent, you make me scared. I thought you fell off the scaffold!' Next day, Malcolm, with yellow thread and black thread, he makes a bee and stick on my flower. Was good."

These stories serve as emblems of the perfection and the realism that carvers strive to attain. To carve flowers that fool the bees is the ultimate achievement. "Our goal is to imitate nature, to make the stone look like real," Vincent told me. "You have to be able to imitate reality."

Much of the pleasure that stone carvers derive from their work lies in the freedom and discipline involved in the art of imitating to perfection "some hitherto-existing reality."[34] Vincent expressed it this way: "I like carving flowers, especially roses, because carving flowers you are completely free. You can twist the petals of the flowers so harmoniously. In other words, it's a challenge with the nature and the hardness of stone to make the stone look like real. You've got to know how to give that feeling—even if it is on stone—that the flowers move. That's the challenge between the man working the stone and the nature of the flower. And that's very difficult. Not too many can give that touch on stone."

But realism is not the only standard by which beauty and excellence are judged. Accuracy—in the sense of being faithful to the prototype design—is also a major criterion for evaluating performance. Good carvers, like a good ballad singer or a good teller of epic tales, respect the integrity of the original text. They do not change the structure or content of the work, but they can give it life and expression through their interpretive abilities and skills.[35] "You can't judge a carver just because he can carve directly on stone. That does not make a great carver," said Vincent. "There are no rules to follow, no perfection to strive for, no measurements. No way to stop you, what you do."

"You have to have the ability to understand and interpret each different sculptor's style," said Roger. "You have to change your own technique to please the sculptor. I had to change my way of carving to interpret their way. And I have to reproduce exactly what they put there in clay. A lot of carvers let their own egos run away. They think, 'Well, I can do it better.' But that's not the idea. You've got to restrain yourself and be sure that you do what's in the model, that you copy the model to perfection." As an example, Roger described a tribute he had received from one of the sculptors he had worked for in New York City: "He said to me, 'What do you think I want in my model?' I said, 'Well, from what I can see, you don't want anything sharp; you want everything soft and blend in with the background.' So he turned around to Mr. Donnelly [Roger's boss], and he said, 'My God! Don't tell me I find a carver who understands me!'"[36]

Though carvers have a restricted license to interpret, the great carver plays masterfully within these boundaries. Not every carver has these interpretive skills. The great master—the true artist—has a gift. "I think God gives you some of it," said Roger. "It's not all yours. Seventy-five percent God gives you. And then you have to develop it." Reflecting on the qualities of a master, he said, "You have to have the temperament. Your hands has to have a certain feel. You have to have the feel—the certain delicate tenderness. All these emotions contribute to be a good carver. When you carve something, you have to feel it inside you. You gotta know it's got to be soft here, this has to be sharp, this has to be strong. And this you can't learn. Nobody can teach you that."

Through what David Pye has called "controlled freedom in workmanship," Roger and Vincent have created carvings of expressive power and life.[37] Working within set boundaries, they have

White-gloved stone carvers—Vincent Palumbo (crouching at top), Roger Morigi (on the right), and Frank Zic (on the left)—and members of the building crew hoist the completed carving of Adam into place on the Cathedral's west facade. (Photo by Morton Broffman)

endeavored to faithfully translate a sculptor's design into stone, but they have controlled the methods. The outcome has depended entirely on their intent and their skill—on the way in which they have gone about their work. In the end the finished product represents not so much an object as an act—what Robert Plant Armstrong has called "an instance of incarnated experience."

> What we behold in the affecting presence is less of the world of object than a phenomenon of the personal world of man—not a utensil but an act ever in the process of enacting itself—an instance of incarnated experience.[38]

What a stone carver beholds in a finished carving is a "picture of process" imbued with meaning, values, and associations, with memories of artistic action that go far beyond its apparent form and function.[39] "Each piece," Vincent said, "represents a part of my art, my tradition, my family."

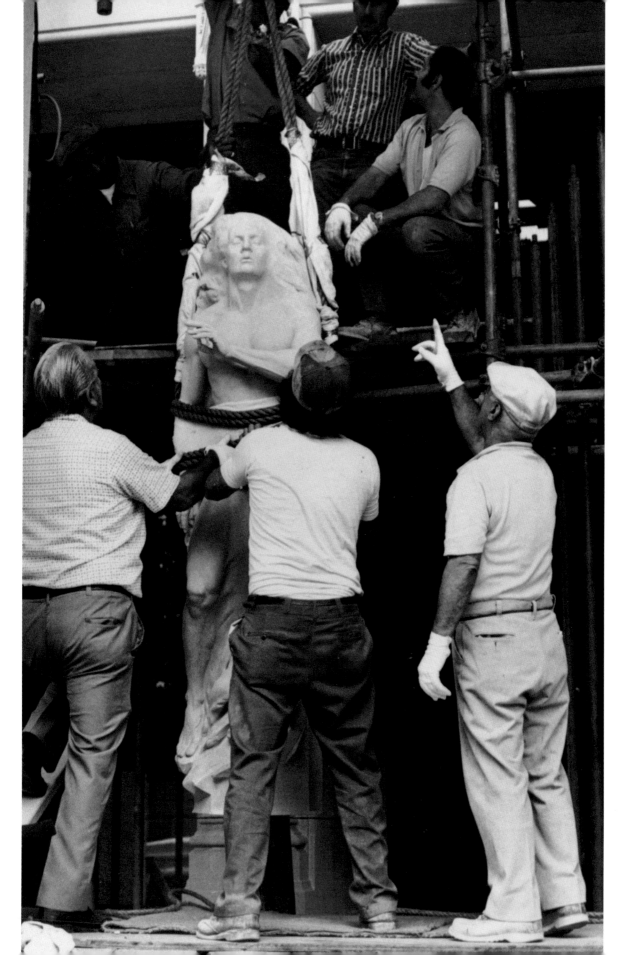

4. STORIES

*There are all different anecdotes connected to the Cathedral,
and we put it all together, and then we put it in stone.*

ROGER MORIGI

tone carvers delight in skill, finding meaning and plea-
sure in the expressive dimension of technique. But in
another body of their work—the freehand carvings
that they design themselves—the primary source of
satisfaction lies less in technique, in ways of working
the stone, and more in content, in the "ideas associated
with form."[1]

"Language is by no means our only articulate product," Susanne
Langer has written in *Philosophy in a New Key.*[2] Stories and memories—vignettes from life experience—emerge on canvas and in wood,
on fabric and in stone. The stories that carvers tell in stone powerfully
evoke a world of work, encapsulating in tangible, enduring form the
experiences, identities, and values of their creators.

Much of the stone carvers' work at the Cathedral involves exactly translating a sculptor's model into stone, but with carvings of a
more architectural nature—pinnacles, corbels, capitals, and especially
gargoyles and grotesques—carvers are often given the freedom to
express their own ideas and imagination.[3] These carvings—fanciful

*Grotesques decorate buttresses supporting the Cathedral's nave. (Photo by
H. Byron Chambers; printed with permission, Washington National Cathedral)*

creations from the carvers' hearts and minds—capture funny incidents on the job; little jokes and stories; memorable characters; the individual attributes, habits, and personalities of the carvers and their fellow workers; or whimsical creations from the carvers' imaginations, inspired by the world around them. "We had a lot of liberty as far as grotesques were concerned," stated Roger Morigi. "When you're carving in any other building, you have to stay more with the architect—certain things go in certain places, and you can't escape from it, you see, because you have to stick to the style and things like that. But in a cathedral like this you have so much freedom."

Wrought from personal experience and handcrafted with the tools and skills of their trade, the stone carvers' freehand carvings are quintessential expressions of the spirit of freedom and responsibility that pervades their work—poignant, powerful statements of individual creativity and shared cultural values.[4] These carvings are also a form of play. Jean Paul Sartre observed that "as soon as man apprehends himself as free and wishes to use his freedom . . . then his activity is play."[5] A source of great pleasure for makers and audience alike, the freehand carvings express the impulse to play that is born in freedom. They exist, as Henry Glassie has written of folk art, "to delight," "to allow man to explore his innovative nature."[6]

In *Rabelais and His World,* Mikhail Bakhtin stressed the "essential relation" between laughter and freedom, noting that an atmosphere of freedom gave rise to the grotesque—an expressive form that he believes is rooted in the culture of folk humor.[7] Among carvers we see that vital relation between humor and freedom manifested in their playful teasing, joking, and storytelling in stone. Infused with laughter, these carvings are expressions of the carvers' pleasure in work—a way to pass the time, to joke, to have fun, and to connect meaningfully with others.[8] "That's the way we pass the life at the Cathedral," said Vincent. "We work, but we have a good time. We have a joke, and the day goes by."

Such carvings embody not only the urge to play but also the impulse to memorialize—to capture memories, experiences, thoughts, and feelings in material, lasting form for present and future generations. These emblems of experience have the power to summon memories, connecting their makers with a significant past, helping

Gargoyle of a scholarly owl, carved by Frederick Hart. (Photo by Stewart Bros. Photographers)

them to deal with the present, and extending them into an unknown future.[9] Constructions of reality, created from personal and social experience, they give their creators, as Henri Focillon has written, "the privilege to imagine, to recollect, to think, and to feel in forms."[10]

A wonderful example is the gargoyle of Roger, designed and carved by John Guarente, a fellow Cathedral carver. Located near the ground on the north side of the Cathedral nave, the gargoyle depicts Roger with his distinctive mallet and chisels—the hallmarks of his trade. A mushroom cloud explosion above his head and a devil's tail and horns signify his notorious temper, and a set of golf clubs carved over his heart denote his favorite pastime. Roger delighted in the gargoyle and enjoyed telling the story behind its creation.

> There was a carver who used to work up at the Cathedral. His name was John Guarente. Now, I always had a quick temper. I blew up real quick. Anyway, he was a good carver with good ideas about gargoyles. So one day I said, "John, go up there and carve that gargoyle." He says, "OK. Look, will you do me a favor?" I said, "OK." He says, "Don't come up here until I tell you to come up here." So I knew that the man was good, and I trusted him and didn't have to worry about it.

So one day he says, "OK, Roger, now you can come up and see it." So I went up there, and what he did, he put *me* up there with a couple of teeth missing, my mouth wide open. And I used to wear a straw hat, so he put me up there pulling the straw hat down with both hands and with an atomic bomb up top here—an explosion of an atomic bomb—and two horns. In one hand a chisel, in the other a mallet. And in back of my behind he put a tail. You see, I was a devil! And in one pocket he put a stiletto and a gun, like a Sicilian in Italy. And on this side here I had tools. And I love to play golf, so over here, next to my heart, he put a set of clubs.

But what he did, at my feet he put a shoe with a hole in it. And on the other foot he put a hoof, a hoof like a cow. You see, the meaning of that is that the devil was always dressed up in high hat, white tie, and tails, but he could never disguise his feet, because [on] one foot he'd have a patent leather shoe, but on the other would be a hoof. And that was the sin, and God condemned him to that. And that's how you can tell the devil, and that's why he put a hoof and a shoe on me. And so I'm up there like the devil!

Above: Gargoyle of a fish, carved by Vincent Palumbo. (Photo by Stewart Bros. Photographers)

Opposite above: Gargoyle of a wild cat, carved by Frederick Hart. (Photo by Stewart Bros. Photographers)

Opposite below: Gargoyle of a winged creature, carved by John Guarente. (Photo by L. Albee)

John Guarente told the following version of the story.

He and I had a little misunderstanding about a week before, so I sort of felt a little bad. It wasn't my fault, but Mr. Morigi can really yodel. So I felt bad. So one day he said, "Go ahead and carve a gargoyle up there." So I was up there, and I'd done quite a few gargoyles before that, and I figured what the heck can I do? But you can't stay there all day and figure what you're going to do, you know, daydream. So I got a piece of tongue and groove board maybe about a foot long by six inches. I said, "You know that son of a gun, he's always yelling. I'm gonna tell the world what he's like."

So I had an idea what I wanted to do. So I started carving this gargoyle, and he would come up maybe once a week or something like that. I didn't want him to know what I was doing because I could get fired for doin' a thing like that, and I had a wife and four little girls to support. But I said, "I'll take a chance, I don't care, and carve that thing." I was so angry. So he came up before it was finished, and I don't know if he knew what it was, but he went down, and when he went down, I finished it up.

On the chisel I put his initials. And he's always blowin' his top, so I have him blowing his top. He has horns, and he's pulling his hat down over his head. In one hand he has a chisel; in the other one he has a mallet. And he has a peculiar mallet, you know, a very odd mallet. And in his back pocket he has a pistol, a bottle of whiskey, and I shoulda put a whip. I shoulda made a whip, to whip everybody. And on the other side, he had calipers in his back pocket.

And then my mother often used to tell me that you can always tell the devil in life; you look at their feet, and the devil has a cleft foot. My mother was Irish, you see, she came from Ireland. And I've seen it in paintings. It's

Opposite: Roger Morigi poses with the Morigi gargoyle on the north side of the Cathedral's nave. (Photo by L. Albee)

Below: The Morigi gargoyle with chisels, golf clubs, and a devil's tail and cloven hoof. (Photo by Robert C. Lautman, courtesy of Marjorie Hunt)

very rare that you'll see that—the devil has one cleft foot. So I made a cleft foot on him, and on the other foot he has a shoe, and he has a hole in his shoe. Then he has a tail, and it goes into a point—the devil's tail. Now what's making him blow his top is that right at his belt is a little gingerbread boy—that's me—that's biting him and making him blow his top.

For John Guarente, creating the Morigi gargoyle was a vehicle for expressing his anger and frustration over a work-related misunderstanding. In poking fun at Roger's fiery personality—in the permanence of stone—John found a playful, creative way to vent his grievance, caricaturing his quick-tempered supervisor for time immemorial.[11]

The Morigi gargoyle is an elaborate portrayal of an individual's personality, occupation, ethnicity, and avocation. We can see the carver's meticulous attention to detail. The mallet in Roger's hand is not just any mallet—it is Roger's "peculiar" mallet—instantly recognizable to all the carvers who worked with him. The gargoyle's hat duplicates exactly the straw hat that Roger wore for many of his twenty-three years at the Cathedral. To everyone who knew him, it was common knowledge that Roger's all-consuming passion, next to stone carving, was golf. Hence, the set of golf clubs carved next to his heart. These carefully crafted details provide the basis for communal remembering; they trigger stories and prompt the reminiscences that flow out of shared knowledge and experiences.[12]

In his caricature John Guarente not only delineated aspects of Roger's personality and occupation but also provided a joking commentary on ethnic identity. Many of the carvers who worked at the Cathedral were first-generation Italian immigrants, hailing from many regions and towns—Tuscany, Lombardy, and Apulia; Florence, Carrara, Lucca, Bisuschio, Pietrasanta, and Molfetta. These craftsmen—Roger Morigi, Vincent and Paul Palumbo, Oswald Del Frate, Gino Bresciani, Edward Ratti, and others—learned their carving skills in their native countries in the context of their families or in the workshops of local masters. They still maintained strong allegiances to their hometowns and spoke their local dialect with family and friends.

A rich part of the carvers' occupational folklife was the friendly rivalry—the stories, jokes, pranks, and sayings—that centered around regional folklore. "Better a dead man in your house than a person from Bari next to you," said Vincent, repeating a traditional saying about the people of his home region. He and Roger described how carvers in the shop would tease Gino Bresciani about his "curious" Tuscan dialect, while the carvers from northern Italy would poke fun at Vincent and his father for their southern Italian foodways and Apulian dialect.

John Guarente captured that playful teasing with regional and ethnic identity in the Morigi gargoyle. By portraying Roger with a stiletto and gun in his pocket, he made a joking reference to the tough guy stereotype of southern Italians. Coming from within the group, and from a fellow Italian American, the detail was, for the carvers, one of the great punch lines of the gargoyle.[13]

Finally, by carving the cloven hoof, traditional symbolism for the devil, John Guarente was speaking to his fellow carvers in a common iconographic language—one that he knew they would understand and appreciate. This sharing of esoteric knowledge contributed to a sense of community for the carvers and was a source of real pleasure and satisfaction, as evidenced by Roger's detailed, enthusiastic description of the cloven hoof.

The stone carvers' tradition of depicting themselves and their fellow workers in stone—of capturing scenes from work and life experience—is a common practice going back centuries in the trade. In *The Gothic Cathedral,* art historian Wim Swaan has described a fourteenth-century carving on the Freiburg Cathedral of a sculptor aiming "his backside in the direction of the Prelate's Palace—the sculptor's protest, so local folklore asserts, against some grievance."[14] Other scholars of medieval art and architecture have noted that images of master masons, architects, carvers, sculptors, and other workers, each depicted with the tools of their trade—chisels, mallets, compasses, carpenter's squares, and the like—adorn the walls and windows of Gothic cathedrals across Europe.[15]

This centuries-old practice has continued right up to the present day. Irish stone carver Seamus Murphy has written that he and his fellow carvers "occasionally indulged in caprice, caricaturizing vice and virtue, enjoying the exaggerated and the fanciful, using as models the odd personalities that were on the job."[16] Tom Murphy, an English

A pinnacle carving depicts Roger Morigi with his beloved golf clubs and the master carver's eagle eye. (Photo by Marjorie Hunt)

A grotesque of Vincent Palumbo exaggerates his curly hair and bushy moustache. He is holding an air hammer in his left hand. (Photo by Robert C. Lautman, courtesy of Marjorie Hunt)

stone carver who worked on New York City's Cathedral Church of Saint John the Divine in the 1980s, noted with satisfaction that "I've had some fun in the gargoyle line. Two of my workmates are on the walls there. They're going to be there, oh, 700 or 800 years. They weren't too happy with that!"[17]

Yet another example from Washington National Cathedral is a carving of Roger's head at the base of a small pinnacle stone, which was crafted by Frank Zic, his longtime friend and associate. Frank depicted Roger with his beloved golf clubs by his side, a stern expression on his face, and the glaring eagle eye of the master carver. This carving portrays Roger in his role as the strict, scrutinizing supervisor and speaks to his working relationship with the other carvers, particularly in terms of status and authority. As caricatures, such carvings have a remarkable capacity for playfulness and parody. Through the visual exaggeration of personal traits, they make comic—yet strikingly realistic—statements about the carvers' lives.

In contrast to the stern, fiery depictions of Roger—the authoritative master carver—is the wide-eyed, open-mouthed portrayal of Vincent, carved by coworker Malcolm Harlow. This grotesque captures the youthful exuberance that characterized Vincent's early days at the Cathedral. "For joke we try to immortalize ourselves, make a caricature of each other," said Vincent of the carvers' practice of depicting their workmates in stone. "As a matter of fact, on the west front there's a grotesque of me, you know, with tools in my hand, my big moustache, and big mouth open, because I used to yell too sometimes."

Malcolm portrayed Vincent with his characteristic carver's cap, curly hair, bushy moustache, and tools. On top of the cap, a carved sketch depicts the story of the time Vincent accidentally bent the Cathedral's flag pole. "We try to make fun, make some jokes, so the day it don't look too long," Vincent explained. Roger especially enjoyed telling the story of Vincent's grotesque, citing it as an example of the fun the carvers had capturing work-related anecdotes in stone and weaving them into the fabric of the Cathedral.

"This is Vincent," he said with a laugh. "In one hand he has his chisels, and in the other he has a pneumatic hammer. You can see on the top of his cap he has a flag pole. Well, up at the Cathedral one day he was going by in his pickup truck, and the wind was blowing, and

A pair of termination moldings carved by John Guarente depict a whistling stone carver and a dismayed dean of the Cathedral. (Photos by Robert C. Lautman, courtesy of Marjorie Hunt)

the rope from the flag pole was flying around, and he caught the rope on his back bumper. And so the pickup truck pulled down the flag pole, and the truck was left hanging in the air! And that's why the carver put this drawing on his cap. And so, there are all different anecdotes connected to the Cathedral, and we put it all together, and then we put it in stone."

The primary audience for these stories in stone is the carvers themselves. Esoteric and traditional, their carvings are key performances of identity and shared experience within a small community—stories "they tell themselves about themselves."[18] To the casual viewer, Roger's gargoyle and Vincent's grotesque appear to be simply fanciful carvings, discernible, perhaps, by some as depictions of stone

carvers, but otherwise largely devoid of meaning. But for the stone carvers, these carvings are richly formulated presentations of self that are filled with multiple associations and meanings. Vehicles for the sharing of firsthand experience and knowledge, these carvings both embody and prompt stories; they stimulate interaction with others and connect the carvers with their fellow workers, friends, and outsiders through storytelling.[19]

A pair of small termination molding carvings located on a flying buttress on the north side of the Cathedral's nave exemplify this playful storytelling in stone. One carving depicts a stone carver on the scaffolding looking down and whistling at the girls. The carving next to it shows the former dean of the Cathedral, Francis B. Sayre Jr., with his hands thrown up in dismay and a look of shock on his face. Roger told me the story behind the carvings.

"[John] Guarente had a lot of imagination. See, he carved a carver cutting the stone, making out like he was on a scaffold out on the building and he was looking down at the girls. And right next to the little gargoyle he carved the dean. And the dean saw the carver looking at the girls, and he's all surprised, you know, he's 'Oh my God!'"

"I was the inspiration of that," Vincent confessed. "I always—I was young, not married, and there were girls—and I'd always look around and whistle. And Guarente said, 'Someday the dean is going to come by and raise you hell!' So, that was the inspiration of that."

This whimsical pair of carvings genuinely delighted the carvers at the Cathedral, and John Guarente—with his imagined outcome to the situation and his creative ability to capture the humor in the carvers' daily working lives—became a heroic trickster figure of sorts, a craftsman who could immortalize the workers' experiences up among the saints and angels that adorn the Cathedral walls. "If we had the freedom, that's what we used to do," said Roger. "Put something in there, you know, to make it interesting. All things like that. It's all around the Cathedral."

Indeed, much of the meaning and fun of these creations comes from the very act of carving them. To be able to express oneself—to incorporate oneself in one's work—is a source of infinite pleasure and satisfaction. The carvings embody and relate stories, but what is more, the act of rendering these anecdotes in stone generates new narratives—stories about creative action that are shared, enjoyed, embellished, and passed down within the workshop community.

Another celebrated story in stone—the telephone conversation pinnacle—is located on the Cathedral's west facade above the central portal. Designed by John Guarente and carved by Frank Zic, it tells of a heated argument between Roger and the then assistant clerk of the works, John Fanfani. "It doesn't make much sense to you, but to us it does," said Roger, pointing to four carved heads at the base of a small pinnacle.

This is one of the pinnacles that goes in the main entrance. There are about ten of them. They take about seven or eight weeks to carve. But what is funny, see all these faces here, all of them, they have a meaning.

I used to have a telephone in my studio, and one day I was working on a figure and the phone rang, and I went over to the phone and answered the phone, and nobody answered. So I hung it up. Two minutes later the phone rang again. I answered the telephone, and nobody answered. So I did that about four or five times. So the last time I answered the telephone, I cussed out whoever it was on the other side in Italian and that was a four letter word!

So about five minutes after came the assistant to my boss, and he's raising holy hell. "Hey, how you talk like that?" he says. "Hey, you don't know who was on the other end." So I said, "Why is it the dummy on the other side didn't answer? I answered the phone four or five times. I've got work to do. I can't be answering the phone like that!"

So one word led to another, and I told him to get the hell out of the place. And I called up my boss, and I told him, "You better come up here in five minutes or you won't find me no more up here!" And sure enough in three minutes he was up there, and I gave him a great big pair of scissors—the kind you clip the hedges. And when he came in there, I showed him the wire to the telephone, and I gave him the scissors, and I said, "Cut!" And he cut. And that was the end of the telephone.

Frank Zic described the creation of the carving this way: "Morigi and Fanfani had a big argument. What happened was, you know when Morigi gets involved in doing something, you've got to say something about Morigi, he really gets involved in his work. There's no question about it. Roger puts his heart and his soul into it. And he doesn't want to be bothered with something. And when the phone kept ringing all day, that infuriated him, and he started to holler, and something happened, and Fanfani and Roger got into an argument. And Roger got so mad he took the phone and ripped it right out of the wall. So we figured we was gonna make something out of that. So we made a little head with a telephone and a cut wire and two guys talking—Fanfani and Roger arguing. We did that. Guarente made a sketch, and I carved it on the stone."

Four carved heads at the base of a pinnacle outline the sequence of events, the characters involved, and the actions taken by each. In the first carving, an enraged Roger yells angrily into a telephone and holds a pair of scissors. In the second carving, on the other side of pinnacle, directly across from Roger, John Fanfani holds the phone to his ear and has a shocked look on his face. "See, this guy here is surprised at what he's hearing," explained Roger. "He's got his hands like that because he's ashamed of the word I said. He didn't want to hear it." In the third carving, the clerk of the works, Canon Richard Feller, looks grave and also holds a pair of scissors. The fourth carving depicts the character who, in Frank and John's imaginations, started the whole misunderstanding—the devil.

This instance of materialized memory is one in a series of small pinnacles located above the west facade's central portal that depict the stone carvers and their coworkers, family, and friends. "There are about ten of these," said Roger, "and each one has a different face—the foreman and the laborer, the engineer, the boss, too. We put Mr. Feller up there. We put Dean Sayre up there, too, in a bigger size than this!"

At the base of one of those pinnacles Frank Zic depicted himself dreaming of deer hunting and winning the Maryland lottery. A wishbone is carved on his left side, a deer antler on his right. Next to him, he carved his friend and fellow deer hunter, John Guarente, holding

Opposite: Cathedral model maker Carl Tucker proudly displays the telephone conversation pinnacle, which depicts an argument between master carver Roger Morigi and his supervisor. (Photo by Marjorie Hunt)

Below from left to right: Details of the telephone conversation pinnacle: an angry Roger Morigi, the shocked supervisor, a grave clerk of the works, and the instigator of the incident—the devil. (Photos by Marjorie Hunt)

an antique muzzle loader in his left hand. Frank also portrayed Gino Bresciani, a stone carver who retired three times from the Cathedral, preparing for his fourth retirement with a bag of money over his shoulder and his suitcase in his left hand.

Malcolm Harlow carved a family portrait of his wife and three children at the base of another pinnacle, along with caricatures of two of the Cathedral's longtime construction laborers, Allen Goodwin and Henry Thomas. Goodwin, who supervised the placement of stones in the stone yard for many years, is portrayed with a chain hoist and dolly. Thomas, a jack-of-all-trades who ran a popular short-order cook house in one of the sheds in the construction yard, is depicted with a cup of coffee, doughnut, hot dog, and piece of pie. Elsewhere on the Cathedral Malcolm carved a grotesque in tribute to all the Cathedral secretaries—complete with telephone, typewriter, and file cabinet—and a caricature of fellow stone carver Patrick Plunkett with his distinctive beard and hat.

Other pinnacle carvings depict Cathedral sculptor and stone carver Constantine Seferlis with the columns and Ionic capitals of his native Greece; Richard Feller, the canon clerk of the works emeritus, with his drafting tools and the mountains of his West Virginia home; carpenter foreman Ludwig Malisky with a hammer and saw; and Walter Fleming, foreman of the Cathedral laborers, holding in his hand a whip that wraps around his head.[20] Taken together, these carvings powerfully evoke a world of work. Esoteric in intent, they represent a special form of in-group communication capable of spinning out into multiple streams of meaning, engaging both the makers and their audience at many different points of entry.[21] Through such carvings the stone carvers present not only themselves but also their culture—commenting on the nature of work relationships, codes of behavior and social interaction, traditions of craftsmanship, and principles of creativity.

One of the carvers' favorite carvings is the golfer's grip gargoyle. Created by Malcolm Harlow, this carving has special significance because several of the carvers, like Roger, were avid golfers. At first glance the gargoyle appears to be simply two hands clutched together. On closer inspection, however, it becomes apparent that the hands are gripped in perfect golfing form and that they bear the markings of golfer's gloves.

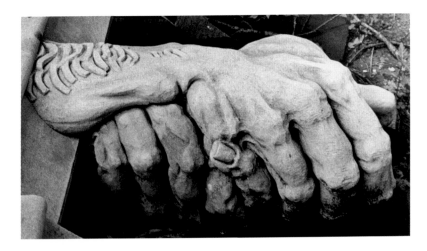

The golfer's grip gargoyle, which immortalizes a favorite pastime of several of the Cathedral's carvers, rests in the stone yard waiting to take its place on the northwest tower. (Photo by Marjorie Hunt)

The carvers continually personalize their work, integrating into their carvings the people who have played central parts in their daily lives. The carving of an angel holding an Oscar, located high on the Cathedral's northwest tower, exemplifies that process. For several years Roger and Vincent worked closely with me on the production of *The Stone Carvers,* a documentary film about their lives and work. To our great excitement, the film won an Academy Award in 1985. A few years later, when Vincent and his crew began to carve the hundreds of angel gablet termination stones that surround eight large pinnacles on the west towers, Vincent decided that he wanted to commemorate the event. Originally each angel was to hold a musical instrument—flutes, oboes, violins, guitars, and the like. "I got the idea," said Vincent, "why does every angel have to carry a musical instrument? Let's put one different. Let's carve the Oscar." Working from a model by sculptor Jay Carpenter, he crafted an angel that bears my likeness, clutching an Oscar in her arms. Thus, I, too, have become a part of the creative process, incorporated into the carvers' stone compendium of experience.

Events in the world also influence the carvers' ideas for many of their freehand carvings. A good example is the hippie gargoyle carved by Constantine Seferlis in the early 1970s. "I thought I should pick one of the extremes of our day," said Constantine of his creation. "And I thought that the hippie would be a good subject to use. It was just all the action of Vietnam and the troubles of those days, and I thought,

Above: Constantine Seferlis carved grotesques of a donkey and an elephant during the 1968 election year. (Photos by Robert C. Lautman, courtesy of Marjorie Hunt)

Left: The lawyer gargoyle, carved by Constantine Seferlis, looks down from the Cathedral's southwest tower. (Photo by Robert C. Lautman, courtesy of Marjorie Hunt)

Below: A buttress gablet termination carving of a television producer, sculpted by Constantine Seferlis and carved by Patrick Plunkett, is located on the Cathedral's southwest tower. (Photo by Robert Shafer ©)

Opposite above: The hippie gargoyle was carved by Constantine Seferlis in the early 1970s. (Photo by L. Albee)

Opposite below: Vincent Palumbo puts the final touches on the Oscar angel, which he carved to commemorate the Academy Award received by The Stone Carvers, *a documentary about the Cathedral's carvers. (Photo by Stewart Bros. Photographers)*

'Well there is so much protesting, so much demonstration going on, why don't we use one of those guys?' And so there is the hippie up there. He's holding his placard, with a pack on his back and holes in his sweater. You see, I thought it would be appropriate to immortalize the hippie of '65 to '72, so maybe in a hundred years you will see in the books the stories about the hippies, but it will be carved on the Cathedral, too."

Other examples include a pair of grotesques depicting a donkey and an elephant, carved during the 1968 election year, and a carving representing the Watergate scandal—symbolized by a stream of water running under a gate—crafted by Vincent during the height of the crisis. Befitting a cathedral located in the heart of Washington, D.C.—a city renowned for its politicians, lawyers, and media personalities—a gargoyle of a lawyer sporting a suit, tie, and briefcase spews forth water on rainy days from a lofty perch atop the Cathedral's stone walls, along with a grotesque of a television producer peering through a video camera.

Stone carvers are not the only artisans at the Cathedral whose art draws on personal experience and events in the world. An English wood-carver, who was crafting the Cathedral's ornate choir stalls during World War II, carved a lion—the symbol of Britain—crushing a snake in its ferocious jaws. On close examination one can see quite clearly that the snake bears Adolf Hitler's signature moustache.[22]

While many carvings capture specific people or events in the carvers' lives, others are simply fanciful creations of imagination, revealing, as Mikhail Bakhtin has written of the grotesque, "an extreme lightness and freedom of artistic fantasy, a gay, almost laughing, libertinage."[23] Those whimsical carvings—flights of fancy and fun—are visible signs of "man's pleasure in labor," produced by the carver, as Henry Glassie has written, out of a "desire to please himself and his audience."[24]

Examples abound. A gablet termination stone carved by John Guarente depicts a lion roaring in anger and pain. If one looks behind the lion, one can see why—John tied a knot in his tail. On the south side of the Cathedral, a grotesque depicts an angry cat, all teeth, claws, and fur; the carving next to it reveals the reason—a fierce-looking bulldog prepares to pounce. On the northwest tower, a gargoyle

Gargoyle of a thief riding a stolen pig, carved by Constantine Seferlis. (Photo by L. Albee)

A host of praying angels surrounds the Cathedral's central tower. (Photo by Stewart Bros. Photographers)

carved by Constantine Seferlis portrays a man riding a stolen pig and holding a chicken in one hand. "We try to be original," said Constantine of his creation.

Another example, a favorite of the carvers, beautifully illustrates the creative license and fun—within certain limitations of form and function—that the carvers had with their work. For the cornice carving beneath the central tower's balustrade, ninety-six angels with overlapping wings and praying hands encircle the tower. Inside the praying hands of one of the angels, John Guarente carved a pair of dice rolling a seven. "Guarente was carving the angels," related Roger, "and the hands

Twin gargoyles of a boy with a broken halo and his hand in a cookie jar, carved by Constantine Seferlis, and a boy with a halo, carved by Vincent Palumbo. (Photos by Stewart Bros. Photographers)

were like that [praying hands], and he carved a pair of dice inside, rolling dice with a seven. And I go in there and say, 'What the hell is that?' He said, 'Oh well, just for a change.' So I said, 'Mr. Frohman [the architect], I would like you to see something.' And he said, 'Oh, that's splendid!' So it's still up there with a pair of dice in its hands."

Sometimes gargoyles and grotesques were created to satisfy the suggestions of specific donors to the Cathedral. Sculptors and carvers enjoyed the opportunities they were given to come up with imaginative ideas for some of those carvings. "You had so much freedom," said Roger. "You're restrained in certain things, but when you come to grotesque things like gargoyles, the more distorted and ugly they look, the better!" He told a story about a pair of gargoyles on the north wall that were sculpted by Carl Bush and carved by Constantine Seferlis and Vincent.

"This fella one time he come up and he wanted to buy some stones for the Cathedral. So we dedicated a couple of gargoyles to his two grandsons—twins. One was kind of wild, and the other was very good. So we put a halo on one and a broken halo and the boy's hand in a cookie jar on the other. Things like that."

"Gargoyles were the best subject we like to work because we were free to interpret any subject we like," said Constantine, talking about a gargoyle he had created for a dentist. "One day a dentist came over and said he would like to have a memorial to his profession. He said, 'I'd like to make a tooth with a cavity.' So we thought that a tooth with a cavity didn't make much sense, so we told the man to come back after a week; maybe we come up with some better idea. So when he came back, he found a dentist working on a walrus, fixing the cavities of the big teeth of the walrus!"

It was not every creation of the carvers' imagination, however, that was allowed to become a lasting part of the Cathedral. Vincent and Roger told the story about one ill-fated carving for a series of patera—small square carvings—underneath the balustrade inside the Cathedral's west front.

"You know when you put me to carve those little things underneath the balustrade over there?" began Vincent. "You know, seventy of those little things. Morigi told me to carve whatever I want, so I started carving flowers, fish, pumpkins, whatever was come into my mind. So I run out of ideas. So I was looking in some books on

A memorial to Cathedral stone carver Joseph Ratti, who died in a fall from scaffolding, was designed by sculptor Heinz Warneke and carved by Roger Morigi. (Photo by Morton Broffman)

fourteenth-century Gothic, and I see some very nasty scenes. So I get an idea. So what I did, I did a man bent over with his pants down and a little bottle [of whiskey] in his pocket. You remember?

"So the dean come up, and he take a look, because Dean Sayre he always enjoy, it was nice, and he stop over there, and he start to look, and he back up a little bit, and he said, 'Vince,' he says, 'what is this?' I said, 'Well Mr. Dean, you know, I run out of ideas and look at some books around here.' 'Uh, uh,' he says, 'Not in this church!' And he went to Morigi, and he said, 'Tell Vince to take off that thing over there.' And so I made a sunflower. I change that, modify it, and make a sunflower from the man bent over."

"That's right," said Roger with a laugh. "The dean came over to me, and he said, 'Did you see what Vincent is doing?' And I said, 'Yeah,' but I didn't know what he did, see. I said, 'He's doing a good job; he's doing a lot of different things.' He said, 'Not the last one! You better go up and check.' So I went up there and said, 'What's that?' I said, 'That's got to go!'"

Though Vincent's carving was modified, the story of his attempted creation lives on in the narratives that carvers tell about their freedom to create from their own imagination and experience. The story—told as an amusing tale about what happens when a carver carries things too far—has become an integral part of the carvers' occupational folklore, preserved and passed down to succeeding generations of carvers.

Filled with human associations, the Cathedral is redolent with sentiment and meaning, with memories and stories from the carvers' world of work. It matters not whether the carvers' creations are free-hand carvings that they have designed themselves or works of translation that bear the mark of their skill, expertise, and care; each piece embodies the identity, values, and thoughts of its maker. Incarnations of experience, they are imbued with memories of artistic action and human endeavor, of fellow workers, friends, and family.[25]

On the Cathedral's north wall two uncarved blocks of stone stand as stark reminders of Joseph Ratti, a carver who fell to his death from the scaffold at that very point. Roger's first carving for the Cathedral was a memorial to Joseph Ratti designed by sculptor Heinz Warneke. Located in the south transept, it depicts a stone carver at

The keystone of Mary Magdalene and Christ was the last carving that Vincent Palumbo and his father worked on together before Paul Palumbo's death. (Photo by Robert C. Lautman)

work on an unfinished gargoyle. For the carvers both the uncarved stones and the memorial keep Joseph Ratti's legacy of craftsmanship alive and serve as constant reminders of the dangers and hardships of their trade.

For Vincent a large keystone of Christ and Mary Magdalene, located on the nave's vaulted ceiling, holds the most tender and precious memories of his father. It was the last piece they worked on together before his father died.

More than a father and son, we were friends. Here at the Cathedral we were for five or six years together, and we become even more close. And especially in the last few months, he and I, we were working on the same piece—it was one of those keystones, huge ones, which is four feet in diameter and represent the conversion of Mary Magdalene. And my father he carved on the ground in the shop; he carved the two figures in the middle, Christ and Mary Magdalene. And all around the circumference of this keystone there is a crown of lilies—lilies are the symbol of purity.

So the masonry was going so fast, they have to set that keystone before my father had the possibility to finish it on the ground. So after they set it, Morigi decided to put my father and I to carve those lilies in situ on the scaffold. So we were working on this keystone, and we started to carve those lilies, and my father was on one side, and I was on the other side, and I was working, and I look at him—how he was doing—and I carved the petals all around, the six petals.

And my father, of course, he was much more fast than I was, and he carved the inside of the lily—all those, what do you call it, membranes, those little stems inside—so gentle, so good, with the drill, with a little chisel. And I was trying to imitate him, but I can't do it. So I went to him, and I said, "Dad, I did the petals of those lilies. Why don't you do the inside because you're doing much better." And so my father carved that one, and I did the next one. In my mind I was thinking to create some kind of assembly line. When I reached the same spot on the lily, I asked him again to do the same thing, but he told me, he says, "Son, I can do it, but you've got to remember, I'm not going to be with you forever. So you better learn how to do." And he make me do the other one. And by golly, I don't know, a couple of months or so after that, he died.

Vincent's deep feelings of attachment to the Cathedral stem from the sentimental memories that are embodied in such carvings. "The Cathedral is a part of me," he told me, "a part of my life."

The carvers' sense of intimacy and connection with the Cathedral is powerfully illustrated by a traditional legend, commonly told among stone carvers and masons, about a carver who had worked at the Cathedral for many years. When his wife died, he asked permission to have her ashes interred in the Cathedral, but his request was denied. He then sneaked into the Cathedral late at night and mixed her ashes with the mortar, thus ensuring that his wife would forever be a part of the Cathedral.[26]

Through their art stone carvers continually incorporate themselves into the fabric of the Cathedral, suspending themselves in "webs of significance" woven from the threads of personality, creativity, culture, and tradition.[27] Indeed, the entire Cathedral can be viewed as a compendium of life and work experience, as a collection of texts that bear the imprint of the carvers' hearts, hands, and minds—"instances of architectural tenderness" left behind for generations to come.[28]

5. MEANING

When you're up in the scaffold, you swing your hammer, and only a little chip comes off the stone. But after years, you marvel how—a little chip at a time—you cut so much stone; you did so much in your life.

ROGER MORIGI

The carvers' beautifully crafted works of art in stone are visible signs of their pleasure in work and their delight in daily skill.[1] Their carvings are not imposed forms, divorced from their makers and their context; rather they are intimately connected to human emotion and intellect. Imbued with personal meaning and associations, they embody both the "freedom of the artist's spirit and the mastery of the artist's hands."[2]

It is this intimate connection to their art that Roger and Vincent have valued most about their work. Through craftsmanship they have had control over the creative process, and thus the aesthetic possibilities of an object have resided completely in their hands. Much has depended on their workmanship and skill: their deep understanding of raw materials and tools, their mastery of technique, and their creativity and care. The final product has been the result not only of their special skills and abilities but also of their attitudes and intentions—their will to excellence.[3]

With freedom comes responsibility. Stone carvers carefully bal-

Cathedral stone carvers Vincent Palumbo, Roger Morigi, Frank Zic, and Constantine Seferlis celebrate together in their workshop at Washington National Cathedral. (Photo by Paul Wagner)

Above: Roger Morigi carves the intricate details of an ornamental canopy with a small air hammer. (Photo by Robert C. Lautman)

Opposite: The trumeau statue of Saint Peter on the Cathedral's west facade was designed by sculptor Frederick Hart and carved by Vincent Palumbo. (Photo by Brooks Photographers)

ance freedom of individual expression with responsibility to community tradition, adhering to the collective values and needs of the workplace. Working within set boundaries, they temper personal creativity with discipline, faithfully translating sculptors' designs into stone, creating works of art that bear the mark of their personalities, technical mastery, and creative spirit.

Roger and Vincent have found satisfaction not only in the freedom and creativity inherent in their craft but also in the infinite variety and challenge of their work. In Gothic architecture, John Ruskin wrote, "there is perpetual change both in design and execution."[4] At work on a monumental Gothic edifice, the carvers' spirits have been "set free" by change. The great diversity of carving—from freestanding statues to bas-relief carvings, from fanciful gargoyles and grotesques to intricate pinnacles and capitals—has kept them constantly challenged and engaged in their craft, giving them opportunities to learn and to grow, to expand their knowledge and to try new skills. "That's the beauty of it," said Roger. "Every day is something different." "You're always learning," said Vincent. "Always it's a different subject, a different kind of stone. Sometimes you feel a little monotony, but you improve all the time; you become a master of that particular piece. You strive for perfection."

The stone carvers have appreciated the time they have been given to strive for perfection. At the Cathedral they have been encouraged to take pride in their work and to maintain high standards—to achieve "perfection and excellence in craftsmanship."[5] "They wanted the very best," said Vincent. "The Cathedral was the best job I ever had," Frank Zic told me. "Everybody knows, that worked there, they wanted a good job. Make it good. They don't care how long it takes. I could do the best I knew how. When you can express your feelings in your work, it makes a lot of difference."

Above all, the carvers have valued the tangible and enduring nature of their craft. "When you're up on the scaffold," said Roger, "you swing your hammer, and only a little chip comes off the stone. But after years, you marvel how—a little chip at a time—you cut so much stone; you did so much in your life, and it's unbelievable. You say, 'My God, look what happened!' You say, 'Look at the tower, look at all the angels, look at the tympanum.' And one day you come around and you say, 'Did I do that?' But the only thing I believe, that we have, the carver has something on top of anybody, because when you're old like me and you look back and you see what you did, you say, 'Well, I did it with my life.'" For the carvers, to be able to behold the work of their hands—lasting creations inscribed with the indelible stamp of their creativity and skill—has been a source of great pride and personal satisfaction.

Through their art, Roger and Vincent have been intimately connected not only to the process of creation but also to their families, their fellow carvers, and their cultural heritage. Stone carving has linked them with their fellow craftsmen, giving them a sense of community in shared work experience and pleasure in the compan-

ionship of others. It has anchored them in a larger whole, binding them to the past through a rich tradition of craftsmanship going back centuries and to the future through their lasting legacies in stone.

It is this vital sense of continuity and connection—to their art, their occupational community, and their heritage—that has given and continues to give meaning and value to the stone carvers' work. Through their mastery and skill, their creativity and care, stone carvers continually incorporate themselves into their art and become one with it. In their lovingly crafted carvings, we see the happy blending of art, work, and life.[6]

A shelf in the stone carvers' workshop at Washington National Cathedral. (Photo by L. Albee)

NOTES

Introduction: Working the Stone

1. "The craftsman's love is materialized in the immanent excellence and patent utility of the things he makes." Henry Glassie, *Turkish Traditional Art Today* (Bloomington: Indiana University Press, 1993), 72.

2. See Lewis Mumford, *Sticks and Stones* (New York: Dover, 1955), 103–6; and Glassie, *Turkish Traditional Art Today,* 108.

3. Unless otherwise stated, all quotations from the stone carvers are from interviews I conducted during my fieldwork. This is a common saying among stone carvers. I have heard similar comments from several of the stone carvers I have worked with over the years. Irish stone carver Seamus Murphy noted that a fellow carver named Black Jack commented, "Didn't we cut the Ten Commandments on the slabs for Moses?" Seamus Murphy, *Stone Mad* (London: Routledge and Kegan Paul, 1966), 19.

4. Raymond Williams, *Marxism and Literature* (Oxford: Oxford University Press, 1977), 115.

5. Ibid., 115.

6. Mark Azadovskii has underscored the importance of exploring the formative forces that influence and govern the generation of folktales. Mark Azadovskii, *A Siberian Tale Teller,* trans. James R. Dow (Austin, Tex.: Center for Intercultural Studies in Folklore and Ethnomusicology, 1974), 12. Folklorist Henry Glassie has argued that in the quest for cultural meaning "what matters is not what chances to surround performance in the world, but what effectively surrounds performance in the mind and influences the creation of texts. . . . Learning what the artists know, learning their history and culture and environment, is one way to reconstruct invisible associations, to pump blood into dry texts." Henry Glassie, *Passing the Time in Balleymenone: Culture and History of an Ulster Community* (Philadelphia: University of Pennsylvania Press, 1982), 521.

7. Henry Glassie, *All Silver and No Brass: An Irish Christmas Mumming* (Bloomington: Indiana University Press, 1976), 57.

8. Henry Glassie, "Folkloristic Study of the American Artifact: Objects and Objectives," in *Handbook of American Folklore,* ed. Richard Dorson (Bloomington: Indiana University Press, 1983), 380.

9. "Style, Grace, and Information in Primitive Art," in Gregory Bateson, *Steps to an Ecology of Mind* (New York: Chandler Publishing Company, 1972), 137.

10. I am indebted to Henry Glassie for his insights on the meaning and value that traditional artists place on the process of creation.

11. Anthropologist Franz Boas recognized the aesthetic dimension of technique in his seminal book *Primitive Art:* "Since a perfect standard of form can be attained only in a highly developed and perfectly controlled technique, there must be an intimate relation between technique and a feeling for beauty." Franz Boas, *Primitive Art* (New York: Dover, 1955), 11–19.

12. John Ruskin discussed the craftsman's delight in skill in his essay "The Relation of Art to Use," in *Lectures on Art* (New York: Allworth Press, 1996), 141.

13. See Glassie, "Folkloristic Study of the American Artifact," 381; and Ruth Bunzel, *The Pueblo Potter: A Study of Creative Imagination in Primitive Art* (New York: Dover, 1972), 1, for illuminating discussions on the way traditional artists balance personal creativity and community tradition. I am indebted to Dell Hymes for his notion of "appropriateness" (*Foundations in Sociolinguistics: An Ethnographic Approach* [Philadelphia: University of Pennsylvania Press, 1974], 94–95, and "Breakthrough into Performance," in *Folklore: Performance and Communication,* ed. Dan Ben-Amos and Kenneth S. Goldstein [The Hague: Mouton, 1975], 16).

14. Robert McCarl, *The District of Columbia Fire Fighters' Project: A Case Study in Occupational Folklife* (Washington, D.C.: Smithsonian Institution Press, 1985), 159–71.

15. Stone carvers regularly engage in what Dell Hymes has termed "true performance," "the taking of responsibility for being 'on stage,' for presenting a genre under circumstances consciously open to evaluation" ("Folklore's Nature and the Sun's Myth," *Journal of American Folklore* 88 [1975]: 352).

16. I am indebted to Henry Glassie for his notion that a completed work of art stands as an "emblem of the creative act" ("The Idea of Folk Art," in *Folk Art and Art Worlds,* ed. John Vlach and Simon Bronner [Logan: Utah State University Press, 1992], 269) and to Robert Plant Armstrong for his concept of art as the incarnation of valued experience (*Wellspring: On the Myth and Source of Culture* [Berkeley: University of California, 1975], 20).

17. Hymes, "Breakthrough into Performance," 18.

18. See Larry Gross, "Art as the Communication of Competence," *Social Science Information* 12 (1973): 115–41; and Kenneth Burke, *The Philosophy of Literary Form* (Berkeley: University of California Press, 1973), 9.

19. I am indebted to Robert McCarl for his insights on the expressive dimension of work technique ("Occupational Folklife: A Theoretical Hypothesis," in *Working Americans: Contemporary Approaches to Occupational Folklife,* ed. Robert Byington [Washington, D.C.: Smithsonian Institution, 1978], 9) and to Henry Glassie for his concept of craftsmanship as the "enactment of values" ("Folkloristic Study of the American Artifact," 376–83).

20. My fieldwork methodology has been informed by the work of Kenneth S. Goldstein (*A Guide for Fieldworkers in Folklore* [Hatboro, Penn.: Folklore Associates, 1964]); Edward Ives (*The Tape Recorded Interview: A Manual for Field Workers in Folklore and Oral History* [Knoxville: University of Tennessee Press, 1980]); and John Collier (*Visual Anthropology: Photography as a Research Method* [New York: Holt, Rinehart and Winston, 1967]).

21. With some outstanding exceptions, in-depth ethnographic studies of traditional craftsmen and craftsmanship in the United States are few. My research has been particularly influenced by the exemplary work of Henry Glassie ("William Houck, Maker of Pounded-Ash Adirondack Pack-Baskets," *Keystone Folklore Quarterly* 12, no. 1 [1967]: 23–54); Ruth Bunzel (*The Pueblo Potter*); Charles Zug (*Turners and Burners: The Folk Potters of North Carolina* [Chapel Hill: University of North Carolina Press, 1986]); Ralph Rinzler and Robert Sayers (*The Meaders Family: North Georgia Potters* [Washington, D.C.: Smithsonian Institution Folklife Studies, 1980]); Charles Briggs (*The Wood Carvers of Córdova, New Mexico* [Knoxville: University of Tennessee Press, 1980]); Michael Owen Jones (*The Hand Made Object and Its Maker* [Berkeley: University of California Press, 1975]); Douglas Harper (*Working Knowledge: Skill and Community in a Small Shop* [Chicago: University of Chicago Press, 1987]); and John Vlach (*A Charleston Blacksmith: The Work of Philip Simmons* [Athens: University of Georgia Press, 1981]).

1. Tradition

1. See George Coulton, *Art and the Reformation* (Oxford: Basil Blackwell, 1953), 199; John Harvey, *Mediaeval Craftsmen* (London: B. T. Batsford, 1975), 45; and Wim Swaan, *The Gothic Cathedral* (New York: Park Lane, 1981), 75. Swaan has written of medieval stoneworkers that "by the fourteenth or fifteenth centuries, fathers would commonly pass on their skill to sons, and many of the higher-paid workers belonged to families long connected to the craft."

2. Raymond Williams, *Marxism and Literature* (Oxford: Oxford University Press, 1977), 115.

3. I adapt words from Dell Hymes, "Folklore's Nature and the Sun's Myth," *Journal of American Folklore* 88 (1975): 346. "[F]olklorists believe that capacity for aesthetic experience, for shaping deeply felt values into meaningful,

apposite form, is present in all communities." I am indebted to Dell Hymes for his concept of tradition as a process—as "traditionalization" ("Folklore's Nature and the Sun's Myth," 353–54). See also Raymond Williams's important discussion of the concept of "selective tradition" in *Marxism and Literature,* 115–18.

4. H. V. Morton, *A Traveller in Southern Italy* (New York: Dodd, Mead, 1969), 130.

5. The *Encyclopædia Britannica* put the population of Molfetta at 57,998 in 1961, the year Vincent Palumbo immigrated to the United States. *Encyclopædia Britannica* (Chicago: University of Chicago Press, 1966), 15: 663.

6. Morton, *A Traveller in Southern Italy,* 117.

7. Jean Gimpel has written that medieval "stonecutters and masons were part of a basically itinerant population of workmen" and that most, by necessity, "led a wandering life" (*The Cathedral Builders,* trans. Teresa Waugh [New York: Harper and Row, 1984], 77–78). For more on the traveling life of medieval stoneworkers, see Coulton, *Art and the Reformation,* 200; Swaan, *The Gothic Cathedral,* 75; F. W. Brooks, "Masons' Marks," *East Yorkshire Local History* 1 (1961), 5; and Douglas Knoop and G. P. Jones, *The Mediæval Mason: An Economic History of English Stone Building in the Late Middle Ages and Early Modern Times* (Manchester: Manchester University Press, 1933), 8.

8. See, for example, Charles Zug, *Turners and Burners: The Folk Potters of North Carolina* (Chapel Hill: University of North Carolina Press, 1986), 287; Ruth Bunzel, *The Pueblo Potter: A Study of Creative Imagination in Primitive Art* (New York: Dover, 1972), 54; and Henry Glassie, *The Spirit of Folk Art* (New York: Harry Abrams in association with the Museum of New Mexico, Santa Fe, 1989), 94–95.

9. Seamus Murphy, *Stone Mad* (London: Routledge and Kegan Paul, 1966), 224–26.

10. See Albert Lord's insightful discussion of the traditional learning process in *The Singer of Tales* (New York: Atheneum, 1974)*,* 21. John James, in his fine study of the stone craftsmen who built Chartres Cathedral, noted that "the individual tended to remain within the mould that had formed him in his early years" (*Chartres: The Masons Who Built a Legend* [London and Boston: Routledge and Kegan Paul, 1982], 141).

11. Henry Glassie, *Passing the Time in Ballymenone: Culture and History of an Ulster Community* (Philadelphia: University of Pennsylvania Press, 1982), 603.

12. Traditionally, stone carvers and masons have been viewed as men of standing in their communities. See Swaan, *The Gothic Cathedral,* 75; and John Harvey, *The Gothic World: A Survey of Architecture and Art, 1100–1600* (London: B. T. Batsford, 1950).

13. E. P. Thompson, *The Making of the English Working Class* (New York: Vintage Books, 1966), 423. George Sturt, in his wonderful autobiographical account *The Wheelwright's Shop,* noted the considerable respect and appreciation that wheelwrights had for sawyers and carters ([Cambridge: Cambridge University Press, 1958], 28–33). Folklorist Robert St. George underscores the importance of examining the networks among craftsmen and their connections to the local community (*The Wrought Covenant: Source Material for the Study of Craftsmen and Community in Southeastern New England, 1620–1700* [Brockton, Mass.: Brockton Art Center/Fuller Memorial, 1979], 14, 18).

14. Edwin Fenton, "Italian Immigrants in the Stoneworkers' Union," *Labor History* 3, no. 2 (1962): 191.

15. Mary Tomasi, "The Italian Story in Vermont," *Vermont History* 28, no. 1 (1960): 76.

16. Fenton, "Italian Immigrants," 193.

17. Ann Banks, *First Person America* (New York: Vintage Books, 1981), 103.

18. Henry Glassie has noted that Turkish potters speak of tradition in strikingly similar terms—as an "atmosphere": "they do not speak of passing things along, but of breathing in the air. You live in a cultural environment, and the air you breathe circulates through you to emerge in actions that are yours alone but can be called traditional because you created them out of the general experience of life in some place. Your works will be like those created by others who breathe the same air. . . . The tradition that binds you is like the air around you, sustaining you, and life within it is comfortable and natural" (*Turkish Traditional Art Today* [Bloomington: Indiana University Press, 1993], 528–30).

19. Doris Fanelli, "Stone Men: Indiana Limestone Craftsmen as Folk Artists" (Ph.D. diss., Indiana University, 1983), 1.

20. Ann Banks has documented several Italian carvers working in Barre, Vermont, who attended the Accademia di Belle Arti di Brera (*First Person America,* 95–119). Many of the stone carvers I interviewed, including Cathedral carvers Frank Zic and John Guarente, had some formal art training in addition to, or as part of, serving an apprenticeship in a carving workshop. Vincent Palumbo's father, Paul, traveled to Pietrasanta, a renowned marble carving and quarrying center in Tuscany, to attend an art academy for six months.

21. Roger Morigi, interview by Virginia Cassiano and Olivia Cadaval, tape recording, Hyattsville, Md., 19 March 1984.

22. The stone carvers and cutters that I have worked with are proud that carvers were among the first workers in the United States to establish a craft union—the Journeymen Stone Cutters Association of North America. Organized in 1853, the Journeymen Stone Cutters Association became affiliated with the American Federation of Labor in 1907 and then amalgamated with the Laborers' International Union of North America in 1968.

23. This version of Roger's story appeared in William Willoughby, "Stone Carver Sees His Art as Vanishing," *Washington Star,* 18 June 1978.

24. Ibid.

25. See Raymond Williams's important discussion of the incorporating power of tradition in *Marxism and Literature,* 115–18; and Henry Glassie's comments on the nature of tradition and the influence of cultural environment on the creative process in *Turkish Traditional Art Today*, 528–30.

2. Learning

1. E. P. Thompson, *The Making of the English Working Class* (New York: Vintage Books, 1966), 253.

2. See Albert Lord, *The Singer of Tales* (New York: Atheneum, 1974), 12, for an important discussion of the nature of the traditional learning process. See also Henry Glassie, *The Spirit of Folk Art* (New York: Harry Abrams in association with the Museum of New Mexico, Santa Fe, 1989), 94–104.

3. Thompson, *The Making of the English Working Class,* 274. For detailed firsthand accounts of the role of the workshop community and time-honored occupational customs in the lives of traditional artisans, see George Sturt, *The Wheelwright's Shop* (Cambridge: Cambridge University Press, 1958); and Seamus Murphy, *Stone Mad* (London: Routledge and Kegan Paul, 1966).

4. Carl Bridenbaugh, *The Colonial Craftsman* (New York: Dover, 1990), 127.

5. Henry Glassie, "Traditional Crafts: A Lesson from Turkish Ceramics," in *Festival of American Folklife Program Book* (Washington, D.C.: Smithsonian Institution, 1986), 73.

6. Roger and Vincent's experience parallels that of medieval stoneworkers for whom the specialization of work processes was largely unknown. See Jean Gimpel, *The Cathedral Builders,* trans. Teresa Waugh (New York: Harper and Row, 1984), 84; and John James, *Chartres: The Masons Who Built a Legend* (London and Boston: Routledge and Kegan Paul, 1982). Charles Zug has described a similar pattern of holistic production for traditional southern potters in rural North Carolina in his excellent ethnography of craftsmanship, *Turners and Burners: The Folk Potters of North Carolina* (Chapel Hill: University of North Carolina Press, 1986), 269.

7. See Lewis Mumford's eloquent discussion of the essential relationship between art and technics in *Art and Technics* (New York: Columbia University Press, 1952), 20–21, 48–50.

8. This point of view is echoed in the written accounts of other traditional craftsmen. See especially Murphy, *Stone Mad;* Sturt, *The Wheelwright's Shop;* and Eric Benfield, *Purbeck Shop: A Stoneworker's Story of Stone* (Cambridge: Cambridge University Press, 1940). John Harvey made similar observations about the training of medieval stone craftsmen in *Mediaeval Craftsmen* (London: B. T. Batsford, 1975), 43.

9. Zug, *Turners and Burners,* 13. See also John Vlach, *A Charleston Blacksmith: The Work of Philip Simmons* (Athens: University of Georgia Press, 1981).

10. See Henry Glassie's discussion of "key texts" in *Passing the Time in Ballymenone: Culture and History of an Ulster Community* (Philadelphia: University of Pennsylvania Press, 1982), 14.

11. David Pye, *The Nature and Art of Workmanship* (Cambridge: Cambridge University Press, 1968), 4.

12. Quoted in Daniel Goldman, "The Vanishing Carver," *Baltimore Sun,* 9 April 1972.

13. Glassie, *Passing the Time in Ballymenone,* 14; and "Folk-

loristic Study of the American Artifact: Objects and Objectives," in *Handbook of American Folklore,* ed. Richard Dorson (Bloomington: Indiana University Press, 1983), 376. See also Sandra Stahl, "Personal Experience Stories," in *Handbook of American Folklore,* ed. Richard Dorson (Bloomington: Indiana University Press, 1983), 268–77.

14. Glassie, *Passing the Time in Ballymenone,* 14.

15. See Erving Goffman, *The Presentation of Self in Everyday Life* (New York: Anchor, 1959); and Mary Hufford, "The Sound and the Story: The Construction and Maintenance of a Canine Symphony" (Ph.D. diss., University of Pennsylvania, 1989), 169. Hufford has aptly described such stories as "self-definitial rites" in *Chaseworld: Foxhunting and Storytelling in New Jersey's Pine Barrens* (Philadelphia: University of Pennsylvania Press, 1992), 35.

16. For further discussion of the importance of speed in workmanship see Glassie, *The Spirit of Folk Art,* 57; and Zug, *Turners and Burners,* 251.

17. For discussions about the respect and status accorded to mastery, see Sturt, *The Wheelwright's Shop;* Murphy, *Stone Mad;* Thompson, *The Making of the English Working Class,* 236–37; and Henry Glassie, *Turkish Traditional Art Today* (Bloomington: Indiana University Press, 1993).

18. The importance of technical perfection and accuracy in craftsmanship is emphasized in the work of other traditional artisans. See especially Ruth Bunzel, *The Pueblo Potter: A Study of Creative Imagination in Primitive Art* (New York: Dover, 1972), 50, 60; and Franz Boas, *Primitive Art* (New York: Dover, 1955), 18. For firsthand accounts of the artisan's concern for accuracy, for "getting it right," see Sturt, *The Wheelwright's Shop,* 53–54; and Ann Banks, *First Person America* (New York: Vintage Books, 1981), 101–2.

19. Glassie, "Folkloristic Study of the American Artifact," 381.

20. Archie Green, "Championing Crafts in the Workplace," in *Festival of American Folklife Program Book* (Washington, D.C.: Smithsonian Institution, 1986), 83.

21. See Robert McCarl, "Occupational Folklife: A Theoretical Hypothesis," in *Working Americans: Contemporary Approaches to Occupational Folklife,* ed. Robert Byington (Washington, D.C.: Smithsonian Institution, 1978), 15–16; and Jack Santino, "Characteristics of Occupational Narrative," in *Working Americans: Contemporary Approaches to Occupational Folklife,* ed. Robert Byington (Washington, D.C.: Smithsonian Institution, 1978), 57–70.

22. Raymond Williams, *Marxism and Literature* (Oxford: Oxford University Press, 1977), 115–16.

23. Dell Hymes, "Breakthrough into Performance," in *Folklore: Performance and Communication,* ed. Dan Ben-Amos and Kenneth S. Goldstein (The Hague: Mouton, 1975), 18.

24. Bunzel, *The Pueblo Potter,* 1.

25. Henry Glassie, *Folk Housing in Middle Virginia* (Knoxville: University of Tennessee Press, 1975), 114.

26. Glassie, *Passing the Time in Ballymenone,* 483; and Mumford, *Art and Technics,* 49. Scholars of medieval stoneworkers have made similar observations about the critical social role of the mason's lodge. See George Coulton, *Art and the Reformation* (Oxford: Basil Blackwell, 1953); Harvey, *Mediaeval Craftsmen;* Wim Swaan, *The Gothic Cathedral* (New York: Park Lane, 1981), 75; and Gimpel, *The Cathedral Builders,* 77–78.

27. Albert Lord has outlined these same steps or stages in his description of the training of traditional Yugoslav epic singers in *The Singer of Tales* (New York: Atheneum, 1974), 21.

28. Tempering is the process of reheating metal—in this case metal tools—to attain varying degrees of hardness, softness, and elasticity.

29. John Ruskin, *Lectures on Art* (New York: Allworth Press, 1996), 57.

30. Glassie, *The Spirit of Folk Art,* 57.

31. Albert Lord's description of the training process for Yugoslav epic singers provides interesting parallels (*The Singer of Tales,* 23–24).

32. Bunzel, *The Pueblo Potter,* 55; and Glassie, "Traditional Crafts," 73.

33. Murphy, *Stone Mad,* viii.

34. In her work with Pueblo potters, Ruth Bunzel observed that creating pottery is viewed as a "vehicle for personal experience. . . . The condemnation of copying the designs of other women is unanimous" (*The Pueblo Potter,* 52).

35. Seamus Murphy has noted that through travel stone carvers "saw what the craft was doing in other parts

of the country and it put them in touch with new methods; they themselves, perhaps, bringing to the workshops
new ways and ideas" (*Stone Mad,* 6).

3. Process

1. All of my descriptions of the stone-carving process at
    Washington National Cathedral are drawn from field ob-
    servations and research I have conducted from 1978 to
    the present. A banker is a workbench used by stonework-
    ers and sculptors.

2. Philip Hubert Frohman, E. Donald Robb, and Harry B.
    Little, of the firm Frohman, Robb and Little, were offi-
    cially designated Washington National Cathedral archi-
    tects in November 1921. After the death of his partners in
    the early 1940s, Philip Frohman continued as the archi-
    tect of the Cathedral until his retirement in 1971. After
    Mr. Frohman's retirement, Howard B. Trevillian served
    as superintending architect until 1981, after which time
    the firm of Smith, Segreti, and Tepper assumed responsi-
    bility. See Richard T. Feller, *Sculpture and Carving at
    Washington Cathedral* (Washington, D.C.: Protestant
    Episcopal Cathedral Association, 1976), 49–61.

3. I am indebted to Henry Glassie for his concept of crafts-
    manship as the "enactment of values" ("Folkloristic Study
    of the American Artifact: Objects and Objectives," in
    Handbook of American Folklore, ed. Richard Dorson
    [Bloomington: Indiana University Press, 1983], 379–80).
    Folklorist Robert McCarl has written extensively on the
    expressive dimension of technique. See especially his
    chapter titled "The Centrality of Work Techniques" in
    *The District of Columbia Fire Fighters' Project: A Case
    Study in Occupational Folklife* (Washington, D.C.: Smith-
    sonian Institution Press, 1985), 159–71; and "Occupational
    Folklife: A Theoretical Hypothesis," in *Working Ameri-
    cans: Contemporary Approaches to Occupational Folklife,* ed.
    Robert Byington (Washington, D.C.: Smithsonian Insti-
    tution, 1978), 3–18. See also Raymond Williams, *The
    Long Revolution* (Westport, Conn.: Greenwood Press,
    1961), 26. Williams has asserted that "the purpose of skill
    is similar to the purpose of all general human skills of
    communication: the transmission of valued experience."

4. See William Morris, "Useful Work Versus Useless Toil"
    and "The Worker's Share of Art," in *William Morris: Se-
    lected Writings and Designs,* ed. Asa Briggs (New York:
    Penguin, 1962), 117–36, 140–43.

5. See Richard Bauman and Charles Briggs, "Poetics and
    Performance as Critical Perspectives on Language and
    Social Life," *Annual Review of Anthropology* 19 (1990): 79.
    For other important theoretical writings on performance
    and communication, see Dell Hymes, "Toward Ethno-
    graphies of Communication," in *Foundations in Sociolin-
    guistics: An Ethnographic Approach* (Philadelphia:
    University of Pennsylvania Press, 1974), 3–27, and
    "Breakthrough into Performance," in *Folklore: Perfor-
    mance and Communication,* ed. Dan Ben-Amos and Ken-
    neth S. Goldstein (The Hague: Mouton, 1975); Richard
    Bauman, "Verbal Art as Performance," *American Anthro-
    pologist* 77 (1975): 290–311; and Roger Abrahams, "To-
    ward an Enactment-Centered Approach to Folklore," in
    Frontiers of Folklore, ed. William Bascom (Boulder, Colo.:
    Westview Press, 1977). Albert Lord's excellent ethno-
    graphic study *The Singer of Tales* (New York: Atheneum,
    1974) also influenced my work.

6. See, for example, Wim Swaan, *The Gothic Cathedral*
    (New York: Park Lane, 1981), 79, 83; and Jean Gimpel,
    The Cathedral Builders, trans. Teresa Waugh (New York:
    Harper and Row, 1984), 60, 77. Swaan and Gimpel have
    documented the central role of the lodge in the work and
    social life of medieval stonemasons. My descriptions of
    the stone carvers' workshop are drawn from field obser-
    vations and research that I conducted from 1985 to 1989.
    After the completion of the Cathedral in September 1990,
    the master carver's studio was converted into an office
    and workshop for the Cathedral's stonemasons, the old
    masons' sheds were torn down, and the size of the stone
    yard was reduced. The main carving shop, where Vincent
    still works today, remains.

7. Gaston Bachelard, *The Poetics of Space* (Boston: Beacon
    Press, 1969), 38.

8. The number of workbenches in the shop has fluctuated
    with the number of carvers and the amount of work. In
    the late 1970s, when I first began my fieldwork, only Vin-
    cent and two other carvers worked together in the shop.
    In 1986, with the push to finish the west towers, Vincent
    had fourteen carvers working for him, with eight benches
    in the main shop. Today Vincent is the only carver re-
    maining at the Cathedral. He works either in the main
    carving workshop or high up on scaffolding on stones
    already set in the Cathedral.

9. Seamus Murphy, *Stone Mad* (London: Routledge and
    Kegan Paul, 1966), 10. See also John James, *Chartres: The*

Masons Who Built a Legend (London: Routledge and Kegan Paul, 1982), 140–41.

10. David Pye, *The Nature and Art of Workmanship* (Cambridge: Cambridge University Press, 1968), 16.

11. Ibid., 1.

12. Henry Glassie, *Turkish Traditional Art Today* (Bloomington: Indiana University Press, 1993), 97.

13. McCarl, "Occupational Folklife: A Theoretical Hypothesis," 7.

14. Giorgio Vasari, *Vasari on Technique,* ed. G. Baldwin Brown, trans. Louisa Maclehose (London: J. M. Dent, 1907), 143.

15. Ibid., 179.

16. Michelangelo described the stone-carving process in similar terms in one of his sonnets:

> The best of artists hath no thought to show
> Which the rough stone in its superfluous shell
> Doth not include. To break the marble spell
> Is all the hand that serves the brain can do.

Ibid., 180.

17. Henry Glassie, lecture on folk art presented at the Smithsonian Institution, Washington, D.C., 11 November 1990. See also Lord, *The Singer of Tales,* 44. Lord similarly has noted that traditional Yugoslav epic singers seek not originality but expression.

18. Franz Boas, *Primitive Art* (New York: Dover, 1955), 25.

19. Ibid., 19.

20. For an illuminating discussion of craftsmanship as the "workmanship of risk," see Pye, *The Nature and Art of Workmanship.*

21. See Feller, *Sculpture and Carving at Washington Cathedral,* 51.

22. Washington National Cathedral is built of 150,000 tons of Indiana limestone. The Matthews Brothers Company and the Bybee Stone Company, Inc., both of Ellettsville, Indiana, served as two of the main stone fabricating plants.

23. Murphy, *Stone Mad,* 19.

24. Quoted in Al Boswell Jr., "Inspiring Journey of a Speculative and Operative Master Mason," *Scottish Rite Bulletin* (Winter 1996/1997): 22.

25. Mihaly Csikszentimihalyi and Eugene Rochberg-Halton, *The Meaning of Things* (Cambridge: Cambridge University Press, 1981), 92. See also Mary Hufford, Marjorie Hunt, and Steve Zeitlin, *The Grand Generation: Memory, Mastery, and Legacy* (Washington, D.C., and Seattle: Smithsonian Traveling Exhibition Service and University of Washington Press, 1987), 43–67.

26. Pye, *The Nature and Art of Workmanship,* 5.

27. For a discussion of measuring devices and techniques, see Vasari, *Vasari on Technique,* 151 and 191.

28. Ibid., 191.

29. J. A. Batchelor, *The Indiana Limestone Industry* (Bloomington: Indiana Business Studies 27, 1944), 116.

30. William Morris, "The Revival of Handicraft," *The Fortnightly Review* (November 1888), 605.

31. Vasari, *Vasari on Technique,* 152.

32. Murphy, *Stone Mad,* 39.

33. Ibid., 26; see also John James, *Chartres: The Masons Who Built a Legend* (London: Routledge and Kegan Paul, 1982), 140–41.

34. See Raymond Williams's discussion of Aristotle and Plato's ideas of art as imitation, as the "representation of some hitherto-existing reality" in *The Long Revolution,* 4. Williams writes: "We speak now of the artist's activity as 'creation,' but the word used by Plato and Aristotle is the very different 'imitation'" (Ibid., 3–4).

35. See Lord, *The Singer of Tales;* Roger Abrahams, *A Singer and Her Songs: Almeda Riddle's Book of Ballads* (Baton Rouge: Louisiana State University Press, 1970); and Henry Glassie, *Passing the Time in Ballymenone: Culture and History of an Ulster Community* (Philadelphia: University of Pennsylvania Press, 1982). For an excellent first-person account of an Italian American stone carver's efforts to follow an original text—in this case a photograph—to perfection, see Ann Banks, *First Person America* (New York: Vintage Books, 1981), 101–2.

36. For a discussion of the way good workmanship carries out or improves upon the intended design, see Pye, *The Nature and Art of Workmanship,* 13.

37. Ibid., 19.

38. Robert Plant Armstrong, *Wellspring: On the Myth and Source of Culture* (Berkeley: University of California Press, 1975), 20.

39. I am indebted to Henry Glassie for his evocative description of a finished work of art as a "picture of process." My thoughts on the nature of the stone-

carving process have been greatly influenced by Henry Glassie's concept of the creation of artifacts as the "enactment of values" ("Folkloristic Study of the American Artifact," 376–83).

4. Stories

1. Franz Boas, *Primitive Art* (New York: Dover, 1955), 12–13.

2. Susanne Langer, *Philosophy in a New Key* (Cambridge: Harvard University Press, 1972), 89. See Mary Hufford, Marjorie Hunt, and Steve Zeitlin, *The Grand Generation: Memory, Mastery, Legacy* (Washington, D.C., and Seattle: Smithsonian Traveling Exhibition Service and the University of Washington Press, 1987), 41. I am indebted to Mary Hufford for her important insights on the nature of memory, culture, and expressive forms.

3. See Richard T. Feller, *Sculpture and Carving at Washington Cathedral* (Washington, D.C.: Protestant Episcopal Cathedral Association, 1976), 14. Canon Feller observed of the Cathedral's many gargoyles and grotesques that "Cathedral carvers have had great fun in creating them from imagination." Francis B. Sayre Jr., dean emeritus of the Cathedral, told me that "the carvers were allowed the freedom to carve their own thing—to express their own ideas. This is what married them in spirit to the Cathedral" (conversation, 12 October 1978). Medieval stone carvers exercised the same creative license with decorative architectural carvings, especially gargoyles and grotesques. See, for example, George Coulton, *Art and the Reformation* (Oxford: Basil Blackwell, 1953), 202, 208. Coulton noted that in many cases the carvers had carte blanche with gargoyles; in other cases the subject was prescribed. He wrote, "So, for his part, the average artist would carve saints to order, but where he was free, he often preferred to carve sinners." See also Wim Swaan, *The Gothic Cathedral* (New York: Park Lane, 1981), 154–56.

4. Henry Glassie, "Folkloristic Study of the American Artifact: Objects and Objectives," in *Handbook of American Folklore*, ed. Richard Dorson (Bloomington: Indiana University Press, 1983), 376. See also John Ruskin, *The Nature of Gothic: A Chapter of The Stones of Venice* (New York: Garland Publishing, 1977), 20. Ruskin observed that the gargoyles of Gothic cathedrals "are signs of the life and liberty of every workman who struck the stone: a freedom of thought and rank in scale of being."

5. Quoted in Mihaly Csikszentmihalyi, "The Rigors of Play," *The Nation,* 17 February 1969, 210. Csikszentmihalyi wrote that "play is the supreme manifestation of human freedom." See also Johan Huizinga, *Homo Ludens: A Study of the Play Element in Culture* (Boston: Beacon Press, 1950), 8. Huizinga argued that the first main characteristic of play is that "it is free, is in fact freedom."

6. Henry Glassie, "Folk Art," in *Folklore and Folklife: An Introduction,* ed. Richard Dorson (Chicago: University of Chicago Press, 1972), 276.

7. Mikhail Bakhtin, *Rabelais and His World*, trans. Helene Iswolsky (Bloomington: Indiana University Press, 1984), 31, 89.

8. See William Morris, "Useful Work Versus Useless Toil," in *William Morris: Selected Writings and Designs,* ed. Asa Briggs (New York: Penguin, 1962), 117, 136; and "The Revival of Handicraft," *The Fortnightly Review* (November 1888): 608. See also Ruskin, *The Nature of Gothic.*

9. I am indebted to Dell Hymes for his important concept of the process of "traditionalization" ("Folklore's Nature and the Sun's Myth," *Journal of American Folklore* 88 [1975]: 345–69). Barbara Kirshenblatt-Gimblett explored the ways in which objects embody and prompt stories in her illuminating essay "Objects of Memory: Material Culture as Life Review," in *Folk Groups and Folklore Genres,* ed. Elliott Oring (Logan: Utah State University Press, 1989), 329–38.

10. Quoted in Barbara Babcock, "Modelled Selves: Helen Cordero's 'Little People,'" in *The Anthropology of Experience,* ed. Victor Turner and Edward Bruner (Urbana: University of Illinois Press, 1986), 320. Clifford Geertz has argued that "cultural forms can be treated as texts, as imaginative works built out of social materials" (*The Interpretation of Cultures* [New York: Basic Books, 1973], 449).

11. Mikhail Bakhtin has asserted that laughter is a liberating force, an effective weapon against both internal and external oppression (*Rabelais and His World*, 90–95). See also Jack Santino, "Characteristics of Occupational Narrative," in *Working Americans,* ed. Robert Byington (Washington, D.C.: Smithsonian Institution, 1978), 70. Wim Swaan offered a medieval example in *The Gothic Cathedral,* 52.

12. Hufford, Hunt, and Zeitlin, *The Grand Generation,* 61. See also Susan Stewart, *On Longing* (Baltimore: Johns Hopkins University Press, 1984); and Kirshenblatt-Gimblett, "Objects of Memory," 329–38.

13. For a discussion of "intragroup" joking with ethnic stereotypes see William Hugh Jansen, "The Esoteric-Exoteric Factor in Folklore," in *The Study of Folklore,* ed. Alan Dundes (Englewood Cliffs, N.J.: Prentice-Hall, 1965), 43.

14. Swaan, *The Gothic Cathedral,* 52.

15. See, for example, Swaan, *The Gothic Cathedral,* 90, 122, 139–42, 154, 242, 281, 309; Jean Gimpel, *The Cathedral Builders,* trans. Teresa Waugh (New York: Harper and Row, 1984), 63, 78, 81; John Harvey, *The Gothic World: A Survey of Architecture and Art, 1100–1600* (London: B. T. Batsford, 1950); and Coulton, *Art and the Reformation.*

16. Seamus Murphy, *Stone Mad* (London: Routledge and Kegan Paul, 1966), viii.

17. Quoted in Suzanne Daley, "Carving the Gargoyles of a Cathedral," *New York Times,* Saturday, 14 May 1983, p. 25. Simon Verity, the current sculptor and carver at the Cathedral Church of Saint John the Divine, recently carved the faces of his friends and coworkers, the local coffee shop owner, and other Harlem neighbors as biblical figures for the cathedral's Portal of Paradise; see Steve Zeitlin, "The Portal of Paradise," in *City Lore* 6 (1997–1998): 4–5.

18. See Clifford Geertz, *The Interpretation of Cultures* (New York: Basic Books, 1973), 448. Henry Glassie discussed the esoteric and traditional nature of folk art in his seminal essay "Folk Art," 253. Folklorist Dan Ben-Amos defined folklore as "artistic communication in small groups" ("Toward a Definition of Folklore in Context," *Journal of American Folklore* 84 [1971]: 13).

19. Kirshenblatt-Gimblett, "Objects of Memory," 329–38. Barbara Kirshenblatt-Gimblett has pointed out that such objects become an important "medium of exchange and focus of interaction—a talking point." See also Hufford, Hunt, and Zeitlin, *The Grand Generation,* 37–67, 89–111.

20. Descriptions of the gablet mold termination stones are taken from notes on those carvings in the Washington National Cathedral Archives.

21. I am indebted to Barbara Kirshenblatt-Gimblett for her ideas about the openness of the visual text in "The Cut That Binds: The Western Ashkenazic Torah Binder as Nexus between Circumcision and Torah," in *Celebration: Studies in Festivity and Ritual,*

ed. Victor Turner (Washington, D.C.: Smithsonian Institution Press, 1982), 136–147.

22. I am grateful to the Very Reverend Francis B. Sayre Jr., dean emeritus of Washington National Cathedral, for showing me this carving and for his gracious help with my research.

23. Bakhtin, *Rabelais and His World,* 32.

24. Glassie, "Folk Art," 266. In his preface to John Ruskin's *The Nature of Gothic,* William Morris argued that "art is the expression of man's pleasure in labour" (*The Nature of Gothic: A Chapter of The Stones of Venice,* ed. William Morris [New York: Garland Publishing, 1977], i.

25. Robert Plant Armstrong has argued that art is "incarnated experience" (*Wellspring: On the Myth and Source of Culture* [Berkeley: University of California Press, 1975], 20). See also Edward Sapir's important article "Culture, Genuine and Spurious," *American Journal of Sociology* 29 (1924): 401–29, for a discussion of art as the "expression of experience."

26. During my fieldwork I have heard several different versions of this legend from various carvers and masons. I have also found three printed versions of the story. See James Wilde, "In New York: Mortar and the Cathedral," *Time,* 25 May 1981, 7; Daniel Goldman, "The Vanishing Carver," *Baltimore Sun,* 9 April 1972; and B. A. Botkin, *Sidewalks of America* (Indianapolis, Ind.: Bobbs- Merrill, 1954), 183.

27. Geertz, *The Interpretation of Cultures,* 5.

28. Geertz has argued that "the culture of a people is an ensemble of texts" (Ibid., 452). I am indebted to Anatole Broyard for the wonderful notion that a stone carving is an "instance of architectural tenderness" ("Cathedrals," *New York Times Book Review,* Sunday, 14 June 1981), 39.

5. *Meaning*

1. My thoughts in this chapter have been inspired and influenced by the writings of John Ruskin, William Morris, Lewis Mumford, and Henry Glassie. See especially John Ruskin, *The Nature of Gothic: A Chapter of The Stones of Venice* (New York: Garland Publishing, 1977), and *Lectures on Art* (New York: Allworth Press, 1996); William Morris, *William Morris: Selected Writings and Designs,* ed. Asa Briggs

(New York: Penguin, 1962); Lewis Mumford, *Art and Technics* (New York: Columbia University Press, 1952), and *Sticks and Stones* (New York: Dover, 1955); and Henry Glassie, "Folk Art," in *Folklore and Folklife: An Introduction,* ed. Richard Dorson (Chicago: University of Chicago Press, 1972), and *Turkish Traditional Art Today* (Bloomington: Indiana University Press, 1993).

2. Glassie, *Turkish Traditional Art Today,* 108.

3. Ibid., 97. See also Mumford, *Art and Technics;* and David Pye, *The Nature and Art of Workmanship* (Cambridge: Cambridge University Press, 1968).

4. John Ruskin wrote that "if, as in Gothic work, there is perpetual change both in design and execution, the workman must have been altogether set free" (*The Nature of Gothic,* 34).

5. Richard T. Feller, *Completing Washington Cathedral for Thy Great Glory* (Washington, D.C.: Washington Cathedral, 1989), 41. Canon Feller writes that "the pursuit of perfection and excellence in craftsmanship has been a guiding light since the first stone was laid."

6. William Morris, "The Worker's Share of Art," in *William Morris: Selected Writings and Designs,* ed. Asa Briggs (New York: Penguin, 1962) 140–43. See also Glassie, "Folk Art," 276–78.

GLOSSARY

BANKER A workbench used by stoneworkers and sculptors.

BOSS A projecting ornament often placed at the intersection of ribs in a Gothic vault.

CANOPY An ornamental rooflike structure above a statue, usually richly carved with small ornaments.

CAPITAL The upper part of a column, pier, or pillar, sometimes richly carved with foliage, animals, or geometric designs.

CLERESTORY The upper part of the nave, transepts, and choir of a church.

CORBEL Stone projecting from the face of a wall to support a beam, vaulting shaft, or piece of statuary.

CROCKET An ornament usually in the form of curved and bent foliage used to decorate the edge of a gable or spire.

FACADE The main exterior face of a building.

FINIAL The topmost portion of a pinnacle, usually sculptured as an elaborate ornament with an upright stem and cluster of crockets.

FLYING BUTTRESS An exterior arched support designed to resist the outward thrust of a building.

GABLET Small gable used as a decorative form on a buttress, pinnacle, or arch.

GABLET TERMINATION Projecting stone at the bottom of a gablet used to conceal molding intersections, often carved with foliage or as a grotesque.

GARGOYLE A roof spout projecting from a gutter to carry rainwater away from the wall of a building, usually carved to represent a grotesque human or animal figure.

GROTESQUE An exterior decorative carving fashioned with monstrous or fantastic features.

KEYSTONE The central stone in an arch.

LABEL MOLD TERMINATION Enlarged stone at the lower end of a molding defining an arch, window, or doorway, usually carved with some form of sculpture or decoration.

NAVE The main body of the church in which the congregation is seated.

PATERA A series of square flowers, heads, or other figures along the underside of a cornice.

PINNACLE A decorative turret tapering upward to the top, enhanced by crockets.

PORTAL A major entrance to a cathedral, emphasized by sculpture and decoration.

REREDOS A decorated wall or screen at the back of an altar.

TEMPER To harden, strengthen, or toughen a metal by application of heat or by alternate heating and cooling.

TRANSEPT Either of the two lateral arms of a cruciform church.

TRUMEAU The central pier of a monumental doorway.

TYMPANUM The recessed triangular space within a pointed or round arch above a portal, usually decorated with sculpture.

VOUSSOIR Wedge-shaped stones that form the curved parts of an arch or vaulted ceiling.

SUGGESTIONS FOR FURTHER READING

Stone Carvers and Masons

Benes, Peter. *The Masks of Orthodoxy: Folk Gravestone Carving in Plymouth County, Massachusetts, 1689–1805.* Amherst: University of Massachusetts Press, 1977.

Benfield, Eric. *Purbeck Shop: A Stoneworker's Story of Stone.* Cambridge: Cambridge University Press, 1940.

Coldstream, Nicola. *Medieval Craftsmen: Masons and Sculptors.* Toronto: University of Toronto Press, 1991.

Harvey, John. *Mediaeval Craftsmen.* London: B. T. Batsford, 1975.

Hunt, Marjorie. "Born into the Stone: Carvers at the Washington Cathedral." In *Folklife Annual.* Edited by Alan Jabbour and James Hardin. Washington, D.C.: Library of Congress, 1985.

James, John. *Chartres: The Masons Who Built a Legend.* London and Boston: Routledge and Kegan Paul, 1982.

Knoop, Douglas, and G. P. Jones. *The Mediæval Mason: An Economic History of English Stone Building in the Late Middle Ages and Early Modern Times.* Manchester: Manchester University Press, 1933.

Ludwig, Allan. *Graven Images: New England Stonecarving and Its Symbols, 1650–1815.* Middletown, Conn.: Wesleyan University Press, 1966.

Murphy, Seamus. *Stone Mad.* London: Routledge and Kegan Paul, 1966.

Stone Cutter's Journal. Official organ of the Journeymen Stone Cutters Association of North America, 1888–1942.

Tashjian, Dickran, and Ann Tashjian. *Memorials for Children of Change: The Art of Early New England Stone Carving.* Middletown, Conn.: Wesleyan University Press, 1974.

Gothic Art and Architecture

Coulton, George. *Art and the Reformation.* Oxford: Basil Blackwell, 1953.

Duby, Georges. *The Age of the Cathedrals: Art and Society 980–1420.* Chicago: University of Chicago Press, 1983.

Eco, Umberto. *Art and Beauty in the Middle Ages.* New Haven: Yale University Press, 1986.

Gimpel, Jean. *The Cathedral Builders.* Translated by Teresa Waugh. New York: Harper and Row, 1984.

Harvey, John. *The Gothic World: A Survey of Architecture and Art, 1100–1600:* London: B. T. Batsford, 1950.

Icher, François. *Building the Great Cathedrals.* Translated by Anthony Zielonka. New York: Harry Abrams, 1998.

Panofsky, Erwin. *Gothic Architecture and Scholasticism.* Cambridge: MIT Press, 1951.

Ruskin, John. *The Nature of Gothic: A Chapter of The Stones of Venice.* Edited by William Morris. New York: Garland Publishing, 1977.

Simson, Otto von. *The Gothic Cathedral: Origins of Gothic Architecture and the Medieval Concept of Order.* Princeton, N.J.: Princeton University Press, 1988.

Swaan, Wim. *The Gothic Cathedral.* New York: Park Lane, 1981.

Washington National Cathedral

Feller, Richard T. *For Thy Great Glory.* Culpeper, Va.: Community Press of Culpeper, 1965.

———. *Sculpture and Carving at Washington Cathedral.* Washington, D.C.: Protestant Episcopal Cathedral Association, 1976.

Harrington, Ty. *The Last Cathedral.* Englewood Cliffs, N.J.: Prentice-Hall, 1979.

Material Culture

Ackerman, James. "Toward a New Social Theory of Art." *New Literary History* 4 (1973): 305–30.

Bachelard, Gaston. *The Poetics of Space.* Boston: Beacon Press, 1969.

Bateson, Gregory. "Style, Grace and Information in Primitive Art." In *Steps to an Ecology of Mind.* New York: Chandler Publishing Company, 1972.

Boas, Franz. *Primitive Art.* New York: Dover, 1955.

Bridenbaugh, Carl. *The Colonial Craftsman.* New York: Dover, 1990.

Briggs, Charles. *The Wood Carvers of Córdova, New Mexico: Social Dimensions of an Artistic "Revival."* Knoxville: University of Tennessee Press, 1980.

Bronner, Simon J. *Chain Carvers: Old Men Crafting Meaning.* Lexington: University Press of Kentucky, 1984.

Bunzel, Ruth. *The Pueblo Potter: A Study of Creative Imagination in Primitive Art.* New York: Dover, 1972.

Csikszentmihalyi, Mihaly, and Eugene Rochberg-Halton. *The Meaning of Things.* Cambridge: Cambridge University Press, 1981.

Deetz, James. *In Small Things Forgotten.* New York: Anchor Press, 1977.

Focillon, Henri. *The Life of Forms in Art.* New York: George Wittenborn, 1948.

Glassie, Henry. "Folk Art." In *Folklore and Folklife: An Introduction.* Edited by Richard Dorson. Chicago: University of Chicago Press, 1972.

———. "Folkloristic Study of the American Artifact: Objects and Objectives." In *Handbook of American Folklore.* Edited by Richard Dorson. Bloomington: Indiana University Press, 1983.

———. *The Spirit of Folk Art.* New York: Harry Abrams in association with the Museum of New Mexico, Santa Fe, 1989.

———. *Turkish Traditional Art Today.* Bloomington: Indiana University Press, 1993.

Harper, Douglas. *Working Knowledge: Skill and Community in a Small Shop.* Chicago: University of Chicago Press, 1987.

Jenkins, J. Geraint. *Traditional Country Craftsmen.* London: Routledge and Kegan Paul, 1965.

Jones, Michael Owen. *The Handmade Object and Its Maker.* Berkeley: University of California Press, 1975.

Joyce, Rosemary. *A Bearer of Tradition: Dwight Stump, Basketmaker.* Athens: University of Georgia Press, 1989.

Kirshenblatt-Gimblett, Barbara. "Objects of Memory: Material Culture as Life Review." In *Folk Groups and Folklore Genres: A Reader.* Edited by Elliott Oring. Logan: Utah State University Press, 1989.

Morris, William. *Hopes and Fears for Art.* London: Ellis and White, 1882.

———. "The Revival of Handicraft," *The Fortnightly Review* (November 1888): 603–610.

Mumford, Lewis. *Art and Technics.* New York: Columbia University Press, 1952.

———. *Sticks and Stones: A Study of American Architecture and Civilization.* New York: Dover, 1955.

Panofsky, Erwin. *Meaning in the Visual Arts.* New York: Doubleday, 1955.

Pye, David. *The Nature of Design.* New York: Reinhold Publishing, 1964.

———. *The Nature and Art of Workmanship.* Cambridge: Cambridge University Press, 1968.

Rinzler, Ralph, and Robert Sayers. *The Meaders Family: North Georgia Potters.* Washington, D.C.: Smithsonian Institution Folklife Studies, 1980.

Ruskin, John. "The Relation of Art to Use." In *Lectures on Art.* New York: Allworth Press, 1996.

Schapiro, Meyer. "Style." In *Anthropology Today.* Edited by A. L. Kroeber. Chicago: University of Chicago Press, 1953.

St. George, Robert. *The Wrought Covenant: Source Material for the Study of Craftsmen and Community in Southeastern New England, 1620–1700.* Brockton, Mass.: Brockton Art Center/Fuller Memorial, 1979.

Sturt, George. *The Wheelwright's Shop.* Cambridge: Cambridge University Press, 1958.

Sweezy, Nancy. *Raised in Clay: The Southern Pottery Tradition.* Washington: Smithsonian Institution Press, 1984.

Vasari, Giorgio. *Vasari on Technique.* Edited by G. Baldwin

Brown. Translated by Louisa S. Maclehose. London: J. M. Dent, 1907.

———. *Lives of the Artists.* A selection translated by George Bull. New York: Penguin, 1965.

Vlach, John. *A Charleston Blacksmith: The Work of Philip Simmons.* Athens: University of Georgia Press, 1981.

Zug, Charles. *Turners and Burners: The Folk Potters of North Carolina.* Chapel Hill: University of North Carolina Press, 1986.

Italian/Italian American Culture and History

Morton, H. V. *A Traveller in Southern Italy.* New York: Dodd, Mead, 1969.

Nelli, Humbert. *From Immigrants to Ethnics: The Italian Americans.* New York: Oxford University Press, 1982.

Noyes, Dorothy. *The Uses of Tradition: Arts of Italian Americans in Philadelphia.* Philadelphia: Philadelphia Folklore Project and Samuel S. Fleisher Art Memorial, 1989.

Tomasi, Lydio, and Madeline H. Engel, eds. *The Italian Experience in the United States.* New York: Center for Migration Studies, 1970.

Tomasi, Mari. "The Italian Story in Vermont," *Vermont History* 28 (1960): 1.

Theory and Method

Abrahams, Roger. *A Singer and Her Songs: Almeda Riddle's Book of Ballads.* Baton Rouge: Louisiana State University Press, 1970.

Agee, James, and Walker Evans. *Let Us Now Praise Famous Men.* New York: Ballantine Books. 1941.

Armstrong, Robert Plant. *The Affecting Presence: An Essay in Humanistic Anthropology.* Urbana: University of Illinois Press, 1971.

Bakhtin, Mikhail. *Rabelais and His World.* Translated by Helene Iswolsky. Bloomington: Indiana University Press, 1984.

Banks, Ann. *First Person America.* New York: Vintage Books, 1981.

Bauman, Richard, and Joel Sherzer, eds. *Explorations in the Ethnography of Speaking.* New York and London: Cambridge University Press, 1974.

Ben-Amos, Dan, and Kenneth S. Goldstein, eds. *Folklore: Performance and Communication.* The Hague: Mouton, 1975.

Briggs, Asa, ed. *William Morris: Selected Writings and Designs.* New York: Penguin, 1962.

Burke, Kenneth. *The Philosophy of Literary Form: Studies in Symbolic Action.* Berkeley: University of California Press, 1973.

Collier, John. *Visual Anthropology: Photography as a Research Method.* New York: Holt, Rinehart and Winston, 1967.

Geertz, Clifford. *The Interpretation of Cultures.* New York: Basic Books, 1973.

Glassie, Henry. *Passing the Time in Ballymenone: Culture and History of an Ulster Community.* Philadelphia: University of Pennsylvania Press, 1982.

Goffman, Erving. *The Presentation of Self in Everyday Life.* New York: Anchor, 1959.

Goldstein, Kenneth S. *A Guide for Field Workers in Folklore.* Hatboro, Penn.: Folklore Associates, 1964.

Hufford, Mary. *Chaseworld: Foxhunting and Storytelling in New Jersey's Pine Barrens.* Philadelphia: University of Pennsylvania Press, 1992.

Hufford, Mary, Marjorie Hunt, and Steven J. Zeitlin. *The Grand Generation: Memory, Mastery, Legacy.* Washington, D.C., and Seattle: Smithsonian Traveling Exhibition Service and University of Washington Press, 1987.

Huizinga, Johan. *Homo Ludens: A Study of the Play Element in Culture.* Boston: Beacon Press, 1950.

Hymes, Dell. *Foundations in Sociolinguistics: An Ethnographic Approach.* Philadelphia: University of Pennsylvania Press, 1974.

———. "Folklore's Nature and the Sun's Myth." *Journal of American Folklore* 88 (1975): 345–69.

Ives, Edward. *The Tape-Recorded Interview: A Manual for Field Workers in Folklore and Oral History.* Knoxville: University of Tennessee Press, 1980.

Kirshenblatt-Gimblett, Barbara. "The Concept and Variety of Narrative Performance in East European Jewish Culture." In *Explorations in the Ethnography of Speaking.* Edited by Richard Bauman and Joel Sherzer. New York: Cambridge University Press, 1974.

Levi-Strauss, Claude. *Tristes Tropiques.* New York: Pocket Books, 1977.

Lord, Albert. *The Singer of Tales.* New York: Atheneum, 1974.

McCarl, Robert. "Occupational Folklife: A Theoretical Hypothesis." In *Working Americans: Contemporary Approaches to Occupational Folklife.* Edited by Robert H. Byington. Washington, D.C.: Smithsonian Institution, 1978.

Stahl, Sandra K. D. "Personal Experience Stories." In *Handbook of American Folklore.* Edited by Richard Dorson. Bloomington: Indiana University Press, 1983.

Stewart, Susan. *On Longing.* Baltimore: Johns Hopkins University Press, 1984.

Thompson, E. P. *The Making of the English Working Class.* New York: Vintage Books, 1966.

Titon, Jeff Todd. "The Life Story." *Journal of American Folklore* 93 (1980): 276–92.

Turner, Victor, and Edward Bruner, eds. *The Anthropology of Experience.* Urbana: University of Illinois Press, 1986.

Williams, Raymond. *Marxism and Literature.* Oxford: Oxford University Press, 1977.

Film Documentation

The Stone Carvers. Produced, directed, and written by Marjorie Hunt and Paul Wagner. Color, 28 min., 16 mm film and 1/2 inch videocassette. 1984. Distributed by Direct Cinema Limited, P.O. Box 10003, Santa Monica, CA 90410. Phone: (310) 636-8200 or (800) 525-0000. Fax: (310) 636-8228.

INDEX